10 ⁸²

LOVE HER...
LIKE HIM

By Pat and Jill Williams

Love Her, Like Him

By Pat and Jill Williams with Jerry Jenkins

Rekindled
Keep the Fire Glowing
Kindling

By Pat Williams with Jerry Jenkins

The Gingerbread Man
The Power Within You

Also by Pat Williams

We Owed You One (with Bill Lyon)
Nothing But Winners (with Ken Hussar)

LOVE HER... LIKE HIM

PAT AND JILL WILLIAMS

Fleming H. Revell Company
Old Tappan, New Jersey

Scripture quotations identified NAS are from the New American Standard Bible, © The Lockman Foundation 1960, 1962, 1963, 1968, 1971, 1972, 1973, 1975, 1977.

Scripture quotations identified NIV are taken from the Holy Bible: New International Version, copyright © 1973, 1978, 1984 International Bible Society. Used by permission of Zondervan Bible Publishers.

Scripture quotations identified PHILLIPS are from THE NEW TESTAMENT IN MODERN ENGLISH, Revised Edition—J. B. Phillips, translator. Copyright © J. B. Phillips 1958, 1960, 1972. Used by permission of Macmillan Publishing Co., Inc.

Excerpt from *What Wives Wish Their Husbands Knew About Women* by Dr. James Dobson © 1975 by Tyndale House Publishers, Inc. Used by permission. All Rights Reserved.

Library of Congress Cataloging-in-Publication Data

Williams, Pat.
    Love her like him / Pat and Jill Williams.
      p. cm.
    ISBN 0-8007-1609-4
    1. Marriage—Religious aspects—Christianity. 2. Williams, Pat, 1940– . 3. Williams, Jill (Jill M. P.) I. Williams, Jill (Jill M. P.) II. Title.
BV835.W548 1988
248.8'4—dc19   88–15311
                                       CIP

Copyright © 1988 by
Patrick L. M. Williams and Jill M. P. Williams
Published by the Fleming H. Revell Company
Old Tappan, New Jersey 07675
Printed in the United States of America

To
Chuck Swindoll
and Jack Wyrtzen
two godly men who have deeply impacted our lives

We are deeply indebted to two special people
who helped us on this book.
Linda Howard was of invaluable assistance
in helping us prepare the manuscript.
Gary Sledge, our editor, has been a source
of encouragement and inspiration on
all our writing endeavors.

CONTENTS

Introduction

Almost six years ago, my wife, Jill, and I began an exciting adventure. The opening scene of this real-life drama, however, had all the ingredients of a tragedy and began with the stark realization that our marriage was over.

I had been happy for ten years—Jill had been miserable. She announced that she could no longer tolerate me, but because of the children and her Christian principles, she would not seek a divorce.

I started a frantic search for the mistakes in our marriage that had made Jill unhappy. I found that God expected certain things from a husband in regard to his wife.

I had completely overlooked the primary principle of marriage, even though it was clearly written in the Scriptures. *A woman must be loved unconditionally, even as Christ loves the Church.* Almost too late, I realized that I must love Jill in the same way that Jesus loves and gives Himself for His body—without reservation or expectation.

This fundamental truth from Scripture has been validated time and again by contemporary psychological research and surveys.

In virtually every popular-opinion poll, women lament that their husbands are not intimate, loving, or open in their communication.

The problem for men seems to be to learn to *love*—to show love, affection, tenderness, and concern for their wives. The problem for women (who frequently say they love their husbands but can't stand their habits, foibles, and behavior patterns) is to learn to *like* their husbands—in other words, to understand the masculine nature, drive, and personal characteristics.

Over the months, as we rebuilt our relationship, Jill threw away the unrealistic fantasy picture of a husband she had embraced since childhood and began to search for ways to like me as a person.

That's why we call our book *Love Her, Like Him.* We want to show husbands how to love their wives as Christ does the Church, and to show women how to learn to accept and appreciate their husbands, even with all their blemishes.

In the years we have ministered to hundreds of couples, we have heard a story repeated again and again. The details vary, but the conclusion is the same.

In our book *Love Her, Like Him,* Jill and I tell the experiences of "Richard" and "Crystal." Although these experiences are based on real people, many of the details we share about their lives have been taken from the letters and testimonies we have heard from couples all across the country. As you read *Love Her, Like Him,* you will understand that the sensitive nature of the details of their lives demands that we protect their identities.

PAT AND JILL WILLIAMS

LOVE HER...
LIKE HIM

Chapter One

Catch the Foxes

The sun caught the reflection of the windshield as a small compact car pulled into the driveway. The rainbow lights bounced off the front window of our house. I glanced out to see who had driven up. Recognizing the car, I wished that Jill were home. I had several important appointments pending and really didn't have time for unnecessary interruptions.

I had dropped by the house in late afternoon to see my wife, Jill, as a lark, a surprise. We had a few minutes together before she loaded up the van and took Karyn, our eight-year-old daughter, to her gymnastics practice. Now wishing I, too, had left, I moaned out loud, saying to myself, "Williams, the last thing you need is this."

Before the young woman could get out of her vehicle, I walked out the front door to greet her. I genuinely liked Crystal, but I didn't have even a second to spare. "Jill isn't home," I said in my most cheerful but important voice, hoping that she'd get the hint that my schedule didn't include surprise visits.

"Hey, Pat, that's okay." *The tone of her voice caught me off guard.* "I'm in a hurry." *I saw her face. Deep pain was etched in her brow.* "Wanted to drop off these color swatches. Tell Jill I'm sorry I missed her." *No, it wasn't pain in her face. A death mask had replaced the usual smile. The muscles in her neck stood out as though she had been under great tension. In sharp contrast, her eyes were lifeless. But it was the steady monotone of her voice that jolted me. I'd heard that tone before. Years before. I'd seen that mask of resignation and defeat on another face — a face more dear to me than life itself.*

"Hold it!" I made my way quickly to her car.

"I have to go." A soft breeze caught Crystal's brown, uncombed hair and softly blew it over her face as she turned the ignition key.

"How are things going?" I asked before she could get the compact into gear.

"Fine."

"How's Richard?"

"All right, I guess. I've left him . . . and I don't want to talk about it."

Just for a moment, I thought that she was going to put the car into gear and bolt from the driveway, but she turned her face toward me instead. "I can't tell you how much I've appreciated all you and Jill have tried to do for us, but I couldn't take it anymore and I've left. That's that, and there's nothing else to say."

I stood in silence. The memories she had churned up from deep within my spirit were still painful—still fresh.

While protesting that she wouldn't discuss her marriage, it was as though a dam of pain and frustration had broken inside her. Crystal gushed on, "I couldn't take Richard's silence and uncaring attitude another day. The only thing that's important to him is his job—his precious promotion. Richard is totally consumed by his work. He doesn't care about me or the children. He never listens. Richard has no time for me.

"I know nothing about *him*. He doesn't share with me. He spends time with the guys from work and church. He hunts. He fishes. He plays softball. But what about me?" Her voice trailed off into a whisper. She stared blankly at the speedometer and absentmindedly brushed dust from the steering wheel.

After a few seconds, Crystal looked at me again. "You know I've tried to reach him." I nodded. Jill and I had been sharing with her for several months. Things had gotten better. Yet it was clear now that Crystal had come to the end of herself.

"Would you give it one more try?" I asked. "Maybe Jill and I could meet with you and Richard." As I mentioned Jill's name, a renewed love for her overwhelmed me. And to think that once I had almost lost her by taking her for granted and by having an attitude of neglect like Richard's. My mind bounced back to a few minutes ago when I watched her getting into the van to take Karyn to her class. She was herding five of our eight children into the vehicle and laughing, waving, caressing, coaxing, joking. Her brown eyes were bursting with life. Jill had been a beauty queen, but she is more beautiful to me today than the day I married her. Her broad smile totally fills her face; she smiles almost all the time.

"I don't know that Richard will come." Crystal's monotone stirred me from my reverie. "He insists that the problem is mine. He doesn't believe that there's anything wrong with him."

"Let's try," I encouraged her.

That evening, Pat told me about Crystal as he and I went over the day's mail. In the stack was a letter from a young professional man who lives in the South, a response to our first book, *Rekindled*.

"Listen to this," Pat said. " 'Donna and I met and were married three months later,' " he read. " 'She became pregnant one month after we were married. I really did not know how to be a husband. Donna and I have been through a lot. We've moved five times in five years. We have never found a place to settle down. Donna, while not emotionally dead, is on the brink of being there.' "

Pat held up the letter. "How many husbands and wives live with the same problems we had?" His voice shook with emotion.

"Couples give up too soon. They feel like they're on a wild goose chase, constantly trying to fix and patch," I said.

"It's more like a fox hunt," Pat mumbled absently.

"What do you mean?"

"Remember The Song of Solomon? The bride laments to the bridegroom,

Catch the foxes for us,
The little foxes that are ruining the vineyards,
While our vineyards are in blossom.

Song of Songs 2:15 (NAS)

"It's the little foxes, the small things of life, that constantly seem to spoil our lives."

In a lot of ways, Pat is the idealistic dreamer in our marriage. Once he grasps the spark of a vision, he pursues it relentlessly. The pain I experienced in the first ten years of our marriage still haunts him. Soon after I was on the road to recovery, he prayed that God would never let him lose the memory of my frustration and hurt. God has answered that unusual prayer to remember the hurt even as we live in the healing.

Now, our life has become a fox hunt, as we cooperate with Jesus in ferreting out the little things in our lives that slowly and relentlessly have tried to destroy us and our marriage. We are also faced daily with "the young professional man from a small southern town" and a "heart-broken housewife who is dying by inches while she busily redecorates the upstairs bathroom."

I called Crystal the next day and arranged for a meeting, and Pat talked with Richard. Crystal had been right. Richard was not interested in getting together with us; but for the sake of "helping poor Crystal out," he agreed to come to our home for a visit.

The evening of the rendezvous arrived, and we sat down at our long, rectangular dining room table. Crystal was pleasant but unexpectant. Richard was confused; his pride had been injured. He wore an air of indifference.

With sympathy and patience, Pat began to share our story with this young couple.

"I was a man driven by success, even though the ultimate goal in my profession was easily within my reach. As general manager of the Philadelphia 76ers basketball team, I was confident that the team would become the 1983 basketball world champions. Even with a photographic memory, I had to work hard to know everything about all the sports. I watched TV incessantly to keep up with the teams, the players, and the scores. Not even the most minute detail of the most obscure team was beyond my interest—the pro and college teams, football, baseball, basketball, soccer.''

Pat explained that experts have proven that success and work can become addictive. The rush of adrenaline a person gets when he is under a great amount of stress is as habit forming as alcohol or cocaine. When he is no longer receiving the emotional high produced by the added surges of adrenaline, the workaholic will become depressed and disoriented.

He actually suffers the same symptoms of withdrawal that any other addict does. The work abuser cannot take a vacation or be away from the excitement and thrill of his addiction any more than a coke user can take a week's break from the powerful drug that occupies his mind, body, soul, and spirit. A man who abuses his work goes from the high highs to the low lows on the emotional spectrum.

Of course, Pat never guessed that he could fit into that category because he was also a peak performer in his spiritual life. He memorized Scripture daily, studied the Bible for an hour each morning, and spoke often, sharing the message of what Jesus could do in a person's life. He ran several miles a day and kept his body finely tuned with health food.

''I did everything a husband was supposed to do—except one thing. I didn't love my wife. Oh, sure, I *thought* I loved her, but I *did* nothing to prove it to her.''

I folded my hands quietly and said directly to Richard, ''I didn't want any of his achievements. I even resented his spiritual accolades. I wanted *him*. I needed his time and attention. I was dying emotionally while he was caught in a whirlwind of activity and spirituality. Even though I didn't know enough then to put it into words, I needed Pat to love me unconditionally.

''Finally, I'd had enough. I'm not sure when the exact point of brokenness came, but one afternoon, I told Pat that even though I would never leave or divorce him, I no longer loved or respected him, and I could never again open myself up to him. My love for Pat had been crushed. We could not have any kind of relationship.''

"I call it D Day," Pat said, placing his hand on mine. "I knew this was not a game. Jill had used a lot of manipulative antics to win a fleeting moment of my attention, but this was different. There was a deadness about her voice and face that terrified me. Suddenly, I knew exactly what I'd lost. I desperately wanted my wife back.

"It seems strange that the moment I realized that Jill no longer wanted or desired my attention, she had it—all of it!''

As Pat shared the story of our marriage, I saw once again that he was stirred by the emotion of those weeks, when he thought he'd lost me forever. Out of a deep fear, he began a frantic search for help. Though he rejected going to a professional counselor because he still had too much pride to admit that he had failed, he began to read. I had a large collection of marriage manuals. But until then Pat had never read any of them because he thought our problems were all in my head.

"Over the course of that horrible week, two wonderful things happened to me," Pat told them. "God gave me a miracle. I saw what I had been and what I had done to Jill. I made a list of more than seventy things that were wrong with our relationship and every one of them fell on my shoulders. God had me write the list, and I was stunned to realize as I read it that each item was something that had been rehearsed for me by Jill over the years.

"Then the Lord led me to a book by Dr. Ed Wheat, *Love Life for Every Married Couple.* From that book the Lord gave me a plan based on Dr. Wheat's simple formula which he called B-E-S-T, an acronym for Blessing, Edifying, Sharing, and Touching.''

Slowly, Pat began the painstaking journey of winning back my love through this plan. Crystal had read our book *Rekindled*, which tells about our marriage and how God rebuilt it. When I had talked with her about it a few months earlier, she was excited to put the BEST plan into action in her own marriage. But tonight as we sat around the large table and talked, she was despondent and unmoved. Richard's facial expressions began to show signs of open hostility toward her, though he sat quietly and listened.

Pat especially understood his defensiveness. After all, he had sat in Richard's place before. He told me later that he knew I was praying silently as he shared with them the drastic changes that have come to pass in our lives.

When Pat finished, Crystal and Richard got into their car and left. As we stood in the doorway and watched them pull away, Pat shrugged his shoulders. We were disappointed that there had been little show of emotion or reconciliation. We climbed into bed, still feeling dejected. Suddenly Pat reached over and took my hand. "Let's pray for Richard and Crystal. I believe God not only wants their marriage to end up on the survival list, but He also wants to do something new through us. We haven't learned everything there is to know about this great mystery called marriage. The Lord may want to teach us something totally new."

Pat's prayer was short, yet pointed. "Father, as You know, Jill and I met with Richard and Crystal tonight. In our eyes, nothing was accomplished, but I believe that you don't want this to be the end of their relationship. Teach Jill and me new things through their marriage. Encourage us to be able to help other couples, like Crystal and Richard, who are hurting."

As I agreed with Pat's prayer, the Lord worked a desire in me to see these young people reunited. I silently pledged to play whatever part God wanted me to in their lives.

Early the next morning, Crystal called. I could tell from her tone that she had been crying, but she was struggling to maintain control. "Last night, I was able to catch a glimmer of hope again," she said. "I'm going back home to Richard this afternoon. He's coming to pick me up."

"He seemed angry last night," I inserted.

"Richard is angry, and I'm hurt and bitter. Our emotions haven't changed. However, we talked it over after we left your house, and we're willing to give each other another try.

"I'm still not sure that our problems can be worked out, but would you and Pat help us? With your marriage, Pat totally changed almost overnight. That was a miracle. A part of me wants to change like that, but another part of me clings to the hurt and rejection. I don't know how to be different. Please help me want to change. Could it be that God is working in our lives in a different way, gradually? We didn't get to this hollow hole of anger and disappointment overnight. I feel it may take a slow healing for us, but I believe that God is large enough to help us.''

I pressed Crystal for a commitment. "Will you and Richard put Dr. Wheat's BEST plan into effect in your lives?''

At this point Crystal couldn't hold back the tears another second. She started to cry—large, deep, wrenching sobs—as though her heart were breaking. "Jill, I have to be honest. Neither of us is ready for that. Richard is so angry. I believe his anger is the reason he buries himself in his work. That way he doesn't have to face his problems or the fact that our marriage is not working. And I'm barely functioning as a person. Is there any help for us?''

Under ordinary circumstances, I would have politely dismissed Crystal, but I remembered the prayer Pat had prayed the night before and my own pledge to try to help them. "Let me discuss this with Pat," I said, trying not to show my disappointment in Crystal's lack of commitment to the plan that God had used to change our lives.

When Jill reached my office by phone and told me about her conversation with Crystal, I also remembered our prayer the night before. Could God be trying to teach us something new and exciting through this young man and woman? "Shall we give it a try?'' The expression in my voice must have betrayed my misgivings because Jill's answer came slowly and with purpose, "It's going to be a challenge.''

"But God is big enough to meet any challenge and to touch any need," I said, trying to reassure myself as much as Jill. During the next months, Jill and I came to see that God is big enough to help any couple who has found themselves on the verge of collapse.

Again and again, we have heard from women who have expressed the same sentiments as Crystal. They say, "I want my marriage to be different. But I feel dead inside. Please help me to want to change." During this learning time, Pat and I quickly discovered that we don't have all the answers. However, we sincerely believe that there are things that can be done by each or either partner to keep love and a marriage alive.

Alcoholics Anonymous teaches that destructive relationships can be compared to a well-balanced merry-go-round. The sickness of each person in the family—husband, wife, children— keeps the carousel moving round and round. If one person dares to step off and refuses to be controlled by the rhythm of the music, the merry-go-round comes to a screeching halt.

Chapter Two

Getting to the Roots

For two days, the crisis which surrounded Crystal and Richard was pushed aside. Because of the daily commitments of our large family, it's easy to get caught up in errands and school schedules.

I was preparing supper late one afternoon when I glanced out the kitchen window. As I dusted the flour from my hands into the sink, I realized that the sun was shining. The day had started with a drizzle, then progressed to a shower. The late afternoon sunshine prompted me to turn to our three girls as they sat at the dining room table doing homework. "The sun shines almost everyday in Orlando," I said, motioning to the brilliant bursts of warm rays that had suddenly flooded the room.

When Pat, the children, and I moved to Orlando, Florida, it was no small decision. The professional basketball team Pat was managing, the Philadelphia 76ers, had captured the National Basketball Association (NBA) title in 1983. Professionally, he was at the top of his career.

After the thrills of the national championship were quieted, it appeared that Pat could coast for a time. But coasting has never been the type of "sporting event" Pat enjoys. Pat's mild-mannered attitude camouflages a hard driving interior. Tall and thin, Pat speaks with an assurance that comes from knowing who he is and where he is headed. He was ready for a new challenge. Because his secret desire had always been to take part in developing a new ball team, his attention was drawn to Orlando, Florida.

Orlando has captured the beat of the Disney spirit. When Walt Disney World opened its ambitious complex over fifteen years ago, the sleepy city of Orlando exploded into a sophisticated metro-center. New avenues and vistas soon materialized that would have seemed impossible before the advent of the theme parks.

One possibility was building a professional basketball team. Pat and I wanted to be in on the ground floor of this adventure. In 1986 we transplanted our family of six children to Orlando (Stephen'and Thomas, six-year-old identical twins from South Korea, had arrived on May 1, 1987). It has been a wonderful time for all of us, especially for the older children.

My thoughts returned to Crystal. She is about thirty-two. Richard is thirty-five. In a multitude of small ways Crystal reminds me of myself at thirty-two. I admire her spunk. Although our life-styles are different, our goals are similar. From my own experience, I knew that this was the most vulnerable time for them as individuals and also for their relationship. The faltering commitment Crystal had made to try to work at her marriage came flashing back to me.

Crystal is a beautiful woman with brown hair falling down her back in waves. Her petite frame can hardly contain the dynamic personality it embodies. Crystal is constantly excited, and when she is happy, she is the most vivacious person in the world. These past weeks had been tumultuous for her. The stress had taken a toll.

Richard is a man whose hands reveal that he is no stranger to work. He is only a few inches taller than Crystal, but he has the bulging muscles that come from long hours on a construction crew. Because of a learning disability, he has little education, but he makes up for it in street smarts. He has been more successful than most men his age who have college degrees. He now has a good position in the front office of one of the largest construction firms in the state.

I checked my watch and realized that Pat and the three younger boys would come bounding through the door in about fifteen minutes. I had no time to call Crystal and talk with her.

After our evening meal, the phone rang. I was pleased to hear Crystal's familiar voice on the other end. Her voice was steady. "Jill, have you and Pat had time to talk about helping Richard and me?" I hated to admit that we had been pressed into other obligations which had left us with no time to talk about them. I hung up the phone feeling a bit down. It had been two days, and Pat and I had not discussed Crystal and Richard. Would we be able to help them after all?

"Are you all right?" Pat asked, sensing my concern. "Who was on the phone?"

"Pat, I could cry. It was Crystal, and she was wondering if we'd had time to discuss helping them. With everything that's been stirring during these past days, I'd almost forgotten them."

About that time one of the twins, seven-year-old Stephen, came into the room and started to tug at Pat's pants leg. "Let me get the children tucked into bed while you finish straightening up the kitchen, and then we'll talk," Pat said with a reassuring grin. I smiled as Pat herded the four smaller children into their bedrooms.

Seeing the change that has come into our lives since the Lord rebuilt our marriage has given me hope for any marriage. Over the ten years that Pat and I struggled with our relationship, I had constantly wondered how a man could be so conscientious, caring, creative, and committed to his job and then mess things up so badly at home.

Unfortunately, with all my nagging and frustration, I had merely been scratching at the symptoms—symptoms that only proved we were not succeeding in our commitment to each other. I had not gotten at the root of the problem. Thinking that the entire matter would be settled once Pat understood that I wasn't getting enough of his attention prevented me from realizing that tugging at symptoms would never heal the hurts or relieve the pain.

As I reached into the freezer for tomorrow's luncheon meat, I saw a package of frozen blackberries. Pat had come back into the kitchen and started to spread the bread with mayonnaise.

"Remember Julie and her blackberries?" I asked, pulling out the frozen bag as a reminder. We both chuckled as we thought about the awful situation our friend had gotten herself into.

Julie loved blackberries, and so she had planted four bushes in her backyard. Not understanding the Florida semitropical growing seasons or the root structure of the plant, she nursed, fertilized, and watered them, working hard to get them to flourish.

To her surprise, before the end of the year, blackberry plants were sprouting up all over the yard. They didn't politely confine themselves to the garden plot; they shot up wherever they chose— in the middle of the lawn, next to the house, in the cracks of the sidewalk. No cranny was sacred. Julie woke up to the reality that she had nurtured a monstrous network of uncontrollable vined varmints.

Because she hadn't reckoned with the thorns before she planted the blackberries, she had been constantly amazed by the masses of pricks and prickles that she and her family endured every time they tried to prune the plants.

Finally, in desperation Julie donned her heaviest pair of work gloves and coveralls and proceeded to dig up the plants. She had no idea that it would be impossible to get to the whole root system, however. In fact, once the mother bushes were gone, the new volunteers only sprouted more profusely. It seemed that daily she was struggling to keep the pesky plants from another unwanted area.

She did get rid of her thorny problem, though, when they put in a swimming pool and covered the rest of the backyard with a concrete slab.

"Most marriage problems are like Julie's blackberries, aren't they?" Pat commented. "Nagging, pouting, and anger only accomplish one thing: They provide fertile ground for more problems to sprout."

In the early years of our marriage, it seemed that Pat was a master at finding ways to show me that his professional career was more important to him than I was. I pulled up the thorny plants of indifference in one spot only to find that they had sprouted in five other areas. I needed to get to the roots, and I couldn't. In utter despair, I allowed my heart to become as indifferent as Julie's concrete slab.

Pat started to put the sandwiches in the brown paper bags. "Jill, I believe that the Lord has given me some specific direction about how we can help Crystal and Richard. Do you think we could meet with them again?"

"It won't hurt to try," I said, reaching for the telephone. Richard answered and was receptive to meeting with us. They had gotten a sitter for the children and were headed out the door to run an errand. He agreed to stop by the house for a few minutes.

Later, they told us that they had both been hesitant to spend time with us. "I won't have them pushing any kind of religious marriage garbage down my throat," Richard said defensively. Crystal was nervous and concerned that Richard would explode.

Once they arrived, Pat and I could sense the tension in them. Pat ignored their nervousness and took the lead, while I prayed silently. "Richard, I've been praying for you and Crystal since the other night, and I believe that God has shown me two things which are necessary for you. First—and this is simple—you must recognize the root of your problems. Then—and this will take a great deal of patience and time—you need a plan of action."

Pat looked straight at Richard. Pat's direct confrontation seemed to melt some of Richard's defensiveness. Seeing Richard's change in attitude put Crystal at ease. I could see the tight lines in Crystal's forehead begin to relax. "For almost all women, the secret to happiness in marriage is knowing that they are loved. My loving Jill was the bottom line of the ledger. While the woman is given some specific directions in the Scriptures about submitting, men are commanded to love their wives—as Christ loved the Church.

"True, Jill did suffer from a poor self-image, but according to many sociologists, almost all women in our culture have a poor self-image. That wasn't Jill's main problem. It was my acute indifference. When the Lord directed me to make a list of things I did which hurt Jill, I found that I was saying in seventy different ways, 'I don't care about you as much as I care about my job . . . my success . . . sports . . . the team.'

"Jill's needs and desires had taken a back seat to almost everything else in which I was involved. I saw the drastic results of my neglect. Jill was robbed of her joy and even her personality. When I set out to change, God allowed us to plow under the root of our problem.''

Pat shared that John MacArthur, a pastor who has a daily radio program, teaches, ''Men, do you want to have a wife who adores and relishes you, who's secure in you? Then let that wife have the confidence that the whole world knows you love her. If *she* knows that the *world* knows that you love her, there is a tremendous security there. Women need to know they are loved, and they'll know they're loved, not when you tell them they're loved, but when you tell everybody else they're loved.''

Pat pulled a stack of reference cards from his Bible case and related the information on several of them. A survey was conducted on human relations by Edwin Louis Cole, who reported: ''In our survey, the common complaint of all women who wrote that their marriages were unsatisfactory was simply their husband's failure to communicate. Even the single women found it hard to communicate with men.''

A study by the New York State University at New York discovered that one of the most effective buffers against stress for women is to have a male confidant. Initially, the researchers thought women would prefer confiding in another woman, but the findings proved differently.

Lynn Atwater, a sociologist at Seton Hall University, interviewed sixty women who had had affairs outside of marriage. She found that these women called emotional communication the affair's greatest reward. If a partner didn't express his emotions well, listen, and empathize, the women ended the affair.

The study concluded that women have extramarital affairs

mainly because they want deeper emotional intimacy. Research on 150 wives in the United States who have had affairs shows that women regard physical pleasure and variety as important but, unlike men, women don't seek affairs mainly for the sex but for open and honest communication. "Men are always asking me what they can do to prevent their wives from having an affair," says Atwater. "I say, 'Talk to her.' "

Measuring his words in an attempt to be understood, Pat said to Richard and Crystal, "The root of your marriage problems is in two parts: (1) Crystal has an acute, insatiable need to be loved, and (2) Richard desires all the benefits of marriage without ever attempting to meet the needs of Crystal."

Pat explained that men and women view marriage differently. For a man, his marriage is part of a successful football season. His life is a series of sporting events. There are victories to be won, losses to lament. Once the game is won, you might save the newspaper clippings but it's time to move on to the next tournament. Courtship is like another conquest to most men. When the course has been successfully completed on the wedding night, you have other conquests, other teams to challenge and defeat.

This is not to say that marriage is not important to a man. It's his greatest victory, his most prized trophy. With tender loving care, he frequently dusts and polishes the symbol of his victory before placing it back on the shelf.

A woman views marriage like a large family meal. Prepared with loving hands, each ingredient is selected and mixed with care. Sautéed or stir-fried, the richness of the flavors comes in the blending and cooking. The height of the meal, however, is not in the preparation or how beautiful it looks on the plates. True pleasure comes when the family sits at the table and savors the dinner mouthful by mouthful. A meal isn't successful unless it's eaten and enjoyed.

"Crystal, the mature woman recognizes that clearing the dishes from the table and cleaning the messy kitchen are also important, for she has grown to understand that the greatest joys come by paying the highest price."

"I'm confused, Pat," Crystal admitted. "It sounds like you're saying that my problem is that I'm unrealistic about what I expect from a husband.''

"That's right, Crystal. Because of your view of marriage and life, you make demands that no man can meet. You've come into marriage with a Cinderella expectation. You intended to live happily ever after. But in reality, only the Lord Jesus can meet your every desire.''

Drawing from a magazine he had placed on the table in preparation for our meeting, Pat read from an article by Dr. James Dobson, "Create the best marriage possible from the raw materials brought by two imperfect human beings with two distinctly unique personalities. But for all the rough edges which can never be smoothed and the faults which can never be eradicated, try to develop the best possible perspective and determine in your mind to accept reality exactly as it is.

"The first principle of mental health," the article continued, "is to accept that which cannot be changed. You could easily go to pieces over the adverse circumstances beyond your control, but you can also resolve to withstand them. You can will to hang tough, or you can yield to cowardice.

"You may have to accept the fact that your husband will never be able to meet all your needs and aspirations. Seldom does one human being satisfy every longing and hope in the breast of another.

"Obviously, this coin has two sides: You can't be his perfect woman, either. He is no more equipped to resolve your entire package of emotional needs than you are to become his sexual dream machine every twenty-four hours. Both partners have to settle for human foibles and faults and irritability and fatigue and occasional nighttime 'headaches.'

"A good marriage is not one where perfection reigns; it is a relationship where a healthy perspective overlooks a multitude of 'unresolvables.' ''

Pat went over his premise again to be sure that Crystal and Richard understood. "These aren't accusations against either of you," he said. "Jill and I see couples in this struggle every day. We were caught in the same destructive whirlwind for years.

"You must get to the root of your problem. Jill came to the end of herself when she totally gave up. I admitted my problem when I saw what I'd done to her.

"A wife forces expectations on her husband that he cannot satisfy and he, in turn, lacks interest in developing a relationship with his wife."

I looked at Crystal and Richard, hoping to see some expressions of tenderness. Rather abruptly, Richard got up from his chair. He took Crystal's hand. "If accepting our basic problem is the easy part of what you have to share with us, I'm not sure that we're ready to hear your plan." He and Crystal started to walk toward the door. "Give us a few days to digest this."

When they left, I was really disappointed, "Pat, are you sure we're going to be able to help them? They are so hurt. I don't think they're ready for the kind of commitments a good marriage takes."

Pat stacked up the materials he had gathered to share with Richard and Crystal. "We can only help them if they decide they really want óur help. I'll check with Richard on Monday. That's the day I usually see him jogging through the neighborhood."

As I snuggled close to Pat that night after we climbed into bed, he sensed that my pain was caused by knowing that neither Crystal or Richard had wanted to admit they had problems. "Are you all right?" he asked.

"I will be. I'm disappointed." Then, remembering what Pat had shared with Crystal about her basic concern, I chuckled. "Sometimes I still have unrealistic expectations," I said as I turned over and fell asleep.

Chapter Three

An Anointed Plan

The next morning, before I could get out of the house to take the children to school Crystal was at our door. Her daughters are in public school, which starts earlier than our children's school. She had delivered them to their classes. Crystal's eyes were swollen and her hair had not been brushed. "Ride with me," I motioned to her as I grabbed my carryall from the sofa.

Pat had not left for work. "I'll see you when you get back," he said, doing his stretching exercises in preparation for a jog.

As we drove the twenty-minute route to school, the children were talking excitedly about the coming day. It wasn't until I'd dropped them off that Crystal and I were able to communicate.

"I know Pat's right about there being a basic problem with our marriage, and I know that I've played a part in that problem. I'm sorry that Richard and I became testy last night." Crystal stared into space. "It's hard to slam into the reality that the marriage I dreamed about and the husband I've longed for will never be there."

"That isn't exactly what Pat said last night."

"Maybe not, but that's what I heard. Richard is on the edge of an outburst all the time. When he felt that Pat had hurt me, he became protective. Jill, I'm so confused. I don't know what to think. After we got home, we got into another big brawl. At first, he was being protective of me, then he started to attack me."

Silence fell over the van as I made my way through the interstate's traffic. As we pulled into the driveway of our home, both Crystal and I were surprised to see Richard's car. He and Pat were waiting in the house. "I called Richard and asked him to come over. I want you two to sit down and hear the plan I believe God has given me for you. After I explain, you can decide if it's for you or not. But at least hear me out."

Crystal and Richard sat on opposite sides of the living room and didn't look at each other. Pat threw his arm over the back of the couch. I felt as though I was sitting on a pincushion. Crystal and I had become friends through church. Even though she is younger than I, she has a maturity I wish I'd had at her age.

Richard has been successful within his firm, yet he and Crystal are able to make a dollar stretch from Orlando to the Atlantic Ocean. However, money doesn't appear to rule their lives. It's clear that hard work is the controlling factor for Richard.

From the first days of their marriage, Crystal fit easily into the niche of the overachiever's dutiful helpmate. Richard draws great satisfaction from what he is able to build, and Crystal is willing to pitch in wherever possible. She handles her household finances as few women can. Crystal is able to make do or do without.

Lack of money has never been a problem for Pat and me because Pat has always been able to earn a living which is above average, but the satisfaction that both Pat and Richard derive from their occupations is identical.

Crystal's ability to fit into her husband's life-style has endeared her to me. In my opinion, that has always been at the top of the list of things which a woman should strive for in a marriage. Even though there are childish parts of her character, her abilities overwhelm me. To see her being torn apart emotionally hurt me.

I pulled my thoughts back to Pat and the conversation at hand. Richard was asking some heated questions, and Pat was doing an admirable job fielding them. Finally, Pat said, "Look, let's not worry about who's to blame. I want to talk to you about the plan God has given me. Will the two of you listen?"

"Sure we will, why not?" Richard answered for both he and Crystal, even though he hadn't looked at her since she came into the house.

"Let me clarify the situation. You and Crystal don't want your marriage to fail?" They both shook their heads. Crystal stole a look at Richard, but his eyes were fixed on Pat. "You don't feel that you can measure up emotionally to major, radical changes, but you want to work slowly and carefully at rebuilding your relationship."

"Yes," Richard said, again answering for Crystal. I noticed a tenderness in his expression as he stole a glance at her. I hoped that Pat had seen it.

"Though I don't believe that your situation can be handled in a simplistic manner," Pat said, "I think God has given me some insights that can help you to change. You know, in the fifth chapter of James, the elders used oil to anoint those who were sick. The method I believe the Lord showed me comes from the acronym, ANOINT. This method is for those whose marriages are ill and need a slow medication to bring them back to health."

A—Admit that you have problems
N—Notice your areas of need
O—Open up
I—Initiate change
N—Notice your partner's needs
T—Take action and take the time
    to work on your relationship

We have frequently praised Dr. Ed Wheat's BEST principles for saving our marriage. He points out that if even one partner in a marriage is willing to Bless, Edify, Share, and Touch the other, a marriage can be saved. But we have found many situations where neither spouse is willing to go that far. The most common circumstance in a disintegrating marriage is that neither partner is ready or able to reach out to the other.

Tragically, many marriages drift and then fail before either person notices. By the time the problem is recognized, the symptoms are too overwhelming and the pain and resentment too great for the partners to deal with the underlying problem. Our answer has been to have each person focus first on identifying his/her own needs and problems.

Our ANOINT method is an early-intervention method that helps a couple deal with core hurts, not the symptoms. It is designed to help spouses first recognize their own needs, then the other person's needs, and finally take action. This is the method we recommended to Crystal and Richard.

"Once you've confessed the basic root of selfishness in your lives," Pat said, "then you can move on to deal honestly with many areas. Do you think that you would be willing to work on this?"

Suddenly the tenderness I'd seen inching into Richard's expression broke. He started to cry. Not sobs, but tears from a broken spirit. He looked at Crystal for the first time. "Last night when I thought that you were coming down hard on Crystal, something broke inside of me. I wanted to protect her from anything that could hurt her. Then we got into an argument after we left here. With the shock of an electrical current, I realized that the person who has hurt her the most has been me. I don't want to admit it, but I fit the pattern of the workaholic you described last night.

"I lay awake all night. I don't know what I'd do if I lost Crystal." For the first time, he looked at her. "Honey, I love you and I want to make our marriage work."

Crystal looked at him but didn't move from her place. "I love you too, Richard, and I'll try, but there's been so much hurt. . . ." Her voice trailed off to a whisper.

Pat moved over to Crystal and asked Richard to come sit

beside her. He led them in a simple prayer of repentance for their selfishness of the past. Then he asked the Lord to guide the four of us as we worked together to bring His ANOINTed plan into place in their lives. As Pat closed, Richard reached over and took Crystal's hands in his. Tears welled up in her eyes as he whispered, "Crystal, I'm willing to try."

Chapter Four

So How Do I Handle This Mess?

The next morning, I planned to consult with a building contractor who had been working on the redesign of our home. As our family mushroomed last spring, with the arrival of our Korean twins, it became obvious that we had outgrown our once spacious home.

My love for refurbishing older houses had followed me to Florida. It has almost become a tradition in our household to leave house design and decisions in my hands because this area is not one of Pat's talents or interests. In the past five years, he has taken a more active part because he has seen that it's important to me to be able to share those details of my life with him.

However, I've stopped taking offense when he doesn't rush to the wallpaper store or help me make the choice between the pretty blue and purple pansies and the rich, grass cloth design for the back bedroom. I've learned to be happy with bringing home the swatches which I've chosen and getting his final nod of approval.

When we looked for a house in Orlando, we found an array of expensive and beautiful new homes. However, I was drawn to an older place. Situated on the edge of Winter Park on the outskirts of Orlando, it was attractively located, a few seconds from the interstate. The fact that it was out of date and in need of major repair made it all the more attractive to me. One of my greatest joys has been to slowly transform a nondescript house into our home.

The fact that the house was plopped in the middle of several acres, had more privacy than most homes, and was placed by a large lake appealed to me and the children. Even though we are on the fringe of the city, there is lots of space to grow. With the twins' arrival, we became desperate to use a portion of that growing space.

Our contractor wisely advised us to move into another house while the construction was going on. We found a small, ranch-style, suburban home in Maitland. There are only four bedrooms for ten people. The small jokes abound. As our son Jim comments, "Even the roaches are hunchbacked in order to conserve space."

An older section of central Florida, the neighborhood is well established. While this won't be our permanent residence, we've been able to make some permanent friends. Crystal and Richard have been among two of the good friends that we've made during our temporary move.

When Crystal called me two days later, I was amazed at the bounce that was in her voice. She almost sounded like herself again. We talked for several minutes until I had to leave to run errands with the children. Before she hung up the phone, she asked if we could get together. I knew that the bond which was being built between us would grow beyond my just helping her with their marriage.

Suddenly, Crystal's tone changed. She became hesitant, almost childish. "Jill, I've wanted you to help Richard and me, not only because of what God has done for you and Pat in your marriage, but. . . ." There was a long pause, "but also because I admire you. My mother was a Christian, but most of the other examples I've had to follow over the years have shown me what a wife and mother should *not* be. I've seen how you handle your children. I've noticed the joy you have in even the smallest duties of your home life. I'd like to be like you.''

"Crystal," I said, touched by her impromptu speech, "I believe God has put us together to learn a lot of things from each other." Crystal had reached out to me and exposed herself. From that moment, I could see a genuine friendship developing between us.

I had sensed that Crystal had wanted me as a friend who was more than someone to have lunch with or to talk with on the phone. Our time together could mean a stretching for both of us. I needed her friendship as much as she needed mine.

Most of my day is like a taffy pull. My greatest struggle is to be able to maintain a semihysterical composure in the middle of bedlam. Suzannah Wesley, the mother of John and Charles Wesley, is my role model. I admire her ability to take care of eighteen children during the dark days of a depressed Europe in the 1700s. Yet she took time each week with each child. The part of Suzannah's life which I desire more than any other is to be able to work without becoming hassled and harried

Pat and I have seen that each one of our children is a unique gift from God. As wiry as a spindle and just as rugged, with light brown hair, Jim, age fourteen, is discovering the wonders of his early teens in junior high. He has not entered that mute stage of early adolescence but is able to communicate with his friends and the family. He also shares his father's passion for sports.

Bob, eleven, and Karyn, nine, have been introduced to the thrill of stardom through EPCOT—the theme park operated by Walt Disney World. They spent their last Christmas vacation appearing several times a day for two weeks in a show with Carol Lawrence at the American Pavilion. They were on the 1987 Disney Christmas special that aired nationwide on the Disney TV channel.

Bob is small for his age, but he makes up for those inches with a determination that could bite a bullet in half. His brown eyes sparkle, and so does his overdeveloped sense of humor.

Karyn expressed her love for the stage when she was just three years old. She asked to sing a duet with me one night when I was performing before a large audience. Not knowing what to expect, I gave her the microphone. From the moment the audience's attention was turned to her, she was shining. Karyn is never happier than when she can perform before a group of people. In the last year, she has turned her performing instinct to sports. Karyn seems determined to become an Olympic gymnast and has already won several medals in state and regional competitions.

Four years ago, Pat and I adopted two Korean sisters, Sarah and Andrea, who are now seven and eight years old, respectively. Their black hair and eyes, along with their happy disposition, win the hearts of everyone they meet.

One year later, Michael was born. At four years old, he graciously accepts the title of "the boss." His disposition can be summed up in one word, "Smiling."

In July of 1987, two wonderful twin boys arrived from Korea to be a part of our family. Thomas and Stephen are eight years old. We know little about their background. As these two delightful boys have learned and adapted to their new home, their adjustment has been smooth, though not without problems. The joy they give to our home, however, would have to be measured by the buckets full. At least for now, they have made our home complete.

Eight children means that we do laundry, cleaning, and cooking for ten people. While there is a lady who helps with the laundry and someone who cleans once a week, there are days when I crash into bed and realize that I've not talked to one other adult except the cashier at the corner grocery store, and Pat.

I came to realize that even though I'd made many good acquaintances since coming to Florida, I only had a few friends. I welcomed Crystal's interruptions in my day with a short phone call or an impromptu break from the routine.

One Saturday morning, she came bounding into the house with a small package she'd purchased at a neighborhood store. Crystal had noticed that I keep a needlepoint project in my carryall to work on whenever time permits. I especially enjoy them during fourth-grade basketball games when the action on our side of the court slows to a walk. During these long hours, it's wonderful to have a project to divert you from the "agony of defeat."

As Crystal's girls busied themselves with the important matter of searching for Sarah and Andrea in order to play house, their mother plopped herself onto the couch, one leg tucked under her, and emptied the contents of the bag onto the middle of the cushion. She had purchased a needlepoint kit. With the enthusiasm of a student ready to embark on a brand-new learning adventure, she had opened all the packages and had gotten the threads tangled. I looked with disbelief at the confusion of colors and cords. "Now," she said, "what do I do with this mess?"

"Throw it away," I said, "and buy a new one."

"But I like this one, and I want to be able to straighten it out. There was only one of these at the store. I believe that anything worth having is worth working at," she said, flipping a finger through the threads.

"Some things can't be straightened out that easily."

"I know," she said, suddenly serious. "I'm learning that about more things in my life than needlepoint."

I started to carefully untangle the threads—one at a time—while I questioned her. "What do you mean? Are you talking about you and Richard?"

Crystal picked up a small clump of thread and started working on it with me. "I think I'm ready to start on the first part of ANOINT. Jill, it's easy to see Richard's problem areas, but it's agonizing to admit that I have problems."

"Crystal, all of us have deficiencies. Admitting where we can make a change is always the first step toward healing a relationship."

"But Jill, there are some things about my life that you don't know about."

"I realize that. After all, a friendship is like a budding rose. We learn things slowly about each other."

"Well, there are some things about me that almost no one knows about. I never mention my father. There's a reason for that."

"I assumed that your father wasn't living and that your mother is a widow."

"That's true, but you should know about the circumstances which surrounded our life together. Then you might change your mind about me."

In a steely, cold voice totally uncharacteristic of her nature, Crystal began her narrative. "When I was a teenager, I didn't have a normal home life. Almost every week, for three years, from the time I was twelve years old until I was almost fifteen, my mother was beaten by my father. Even though I was never the victim of his abuse, I was a terrified young woman.

"My father had never been normal. Oh, he put on the facade of being a Christian and could con anyone into believing that he was the ideal husband and father. But when we were alone, all the masks were left at the back door. Our life was a torment. No, I make a correction. My mother's life was a torment. I actually knew little of what was going on until the last year he lived at home.

"Mother was determined that I would love Daddy and shielded me from knowing what she lived through. In secret my father was an alcoholic. He was always sober in the morning but drank in secret during the evening. By bedtime, he was a stumbling drunk.

"Mother confronted him one Sunday while riding home from church. How could he continue to live two different lives? He only laughed and said that he enjoyed the feeling of power that alcohol gave him, and he didn't intend to give it up.

"Only one time during the last days that he was living with us did he become angry with me and try to physically harm me. He picked up a vase from the dining room table and headed for the couch where I was seated. My mother was in another part of the house; but before he could reach me, she came from nowhere, literally flying across the room. Mother put her whole body over mine.

"My father was so shocked that he crashed the vase against the wall and walked away. My mother says that I was the only human being he ever loved. With me, he was unusually tender. There were hints all during my early childhood that their life wasn't happy. They argued a lot but stopped if I entered the room or if they felt I could hear the disagreement.

"Things grew slowly worse. One summer, my parents came home from a prayer meeting. Mother was radiant. Daddy took me on his knee and explained that he was going to change and that our lives would be different. I wasn't sure what they meant, but they were happy and that made me happy.

"Then the arguments began again, and the beatings. Mother went to our pastor for help and counsel during the early stages of Daddy's illness. He smiled and gave a simplistic answer, 'If you would learn to submit, your husband would be healed and quit beating you.'

"Mother went home and submitted. Our pastor confessed later that he had no idea of the horrors to which she had submitted herself. Of course, I knew little of the terrors she endured in secret until several years ago when I forced her to share everything with me. I felt that I could never be healed until I knew exactly what she had endured behind those closed doors. I know that she only scratched the surface in telling me these facts.

"It took her weeks before I wore her resistance down, and she agreed to tell me a few brief snatches. Even now, she wonders if it was wise. She doesn't want to harm the tiny shred of mercy I've nurtured for him.

"I had not been blind, however, to many of the disagreements that existed between them. I'd seen him take her hand when they were out in a restaurant and squeeze it so hard that tears streamed down her cheeks.

"Mother told me that she knew what it was like to go to bed and not know if she would wake up the next morning. Jill, you must understand that Mother was not masochistic; she sincerely wanted to follow the Lord. She felt that her pastor was a man of God and that he would give her wise counsel."

I found Crystal's story terrible, but I knew from the pain that filled her eyes that it was true. I reached out and took her hand, which was still untangling the matted thread. "God never intended a marriage relationship to be like that."

"I vowed that I would never allow myself to be subservient to any man,'' Crystal said. ''Richard was everything I wanted a husband to be when we met, but he's changed. My greatest fear is that he will become like my father.''

''Crystal, does your mother know why she stayed with your father during those horrible years?''

''She admits now that she believed that she had to be Daddy's 'saviour.' She honestly felt that one day she would find the magic, wifely key that would unlock his miserable heart and release him to peace, serenity, and joy.

''My mother will tell anyone who asks that God never intended her to live under the conditions she was subjected to during the three years that alcoholism was taking a firm but subtle grip on Dad's mind.

''Do you understand that the word 'submit' sends cold chills up my spine?'' The pain and fear in Crystal's face spoke more plainly than her words.

''But Crystal, submission means 'to come under' in a sense which denotes 'coming into a protected area.' The picture that best describes the word is one in which a husband reaches over to put his arm around his wife to protect her from a cold blast of wind or the onslaught of a sudden downpour. To be submitted means to come to a place of protection—not of degradation and abuse,'' I said to Crystal.

When Karyn and Andrea came into the house for lunch, our conversation ended. They had taken Crystal's girls into the back-yard for a pretend brunch. But when hunger crept in, they came to the back door and clamored for some ''real food.''

I coaxed Crystal into the kitchen with her knotted thread while I prepared lunch. Pat had taken the boys to basketball practice, so we had a young ladies' tea party. Sarah joined us and served the tea and sandwiches.

At 1:30 P.M. Crystal gathered her needlepoint threads and put them back into the bag. She started for the front door. Putting her hand on the door knob, she turned, raised her bag, and asked, ''So how do I handle this mess?''

I knew that she wasn't talking about the tangled threads in the sack but the tangled pieces of hurt and fear bottled inside her heart. Without getting up from my seat, I smiled and said, "Remember ANOINT. The first step is to '**Admit** that you have problems.' "

Walking over to the door, I touched her bag of tangled threads. "You're on your way. You've made a big step."

"I know that my fear of my father's illness and my anger have distorted my reactions toward Richard. They are large problems in my life."

"Crystal, I'm glad that you decided to keep the needlepoint pattern you brought even though it appears to be beyond repair. When it's completed, it will stand as a symbol of your determination to carry through even in the worst of conditions."

" '*When* it's completed. . . .' You are a woman of faith!" Crystal exclaimed as she opened the door. "I'm still saying *if* it's complete." She grinned for the first time in over a week and headed for her car.

"It will be complete," I said, stooping down to look at Sarah, who had joined me at the door.

"Yeah-h-h," Sarah agreed with one thumb up and her black eyes dancing, even though she had no idea what we were talking about.

Chapter Five

Admit Your Problem

That same cold Saturday afternoon Jill met me at the door. She realized that Crystal had shared an important chapter from her life, and she was anxious for me to follow up with Richard, if possible.

"I'm not sure that he's ready for my intervention. I'll give him a few more days and see if he calls me first."

The next morning was Sunday. As I helped Jill and the children out of the van at church, Richard came up to me. He was tapping his pants leg with one finger like a man who had been pushed into a decision. "Guess we can't wait any longer," he said. "Crystal won't let me rest until I make an appointment with you."

"Let's all go to Morrison's cafeteria for lunch," I suggested. "I know Jill could take a break from cooking, and the cafeteria is the only place we can afford to take my tribe." I counted the heads as they filed out of the van. Jill says that she doesn't have to count the children anymore. She instinctively knows when one of them isn't around, but I'm still a counter.

After the church service, we arrived at the restaurant with our usual fanfare. You don't take ten people into a public place and not attract attention. Richard's family made us a party of fourteen. After the three older children had settled into a "private" booth, we pushed several tables together to seat the rest of our families.

An avid reader, I'm always interested in any stories that can help to illustrate the problems we face in our daily lives. That morning during my devotions, I'd read an article which had fascinated me. I shared it with Richard and Crystal.

During the time that Magellan made his way around the world, another journey was being made. Though not recorded in many history books, the sojourn of a young university student on foot began an encounter with destiny that would set off shock waves within the Church throughout the continent of Europe and continue to reverberate for another century. Martin Luther's encounter with a personal God had an impact which would continue until all of Europe had been reshaped.

It was a blistering, hot July day when the brilliant young university student made his short jaunt to the small town where he was enrolled in law school. At twenty-one, his mind was saturated with the classics and scholastic debate. Born to middle-class parents, the student was aware of the hardships that had been endured to allow him to have the best education.

His parents (especially his father) were sure that their son would one day have a distinguished career, perhaps as a city magistrate, a counselor in court, or a district manager. No one except God could have guessed how wrong all these parental aspirations were.

Foreboding dark clouds loomed in the July sky over the path to Erfurt, Germany, as Luther trudged his way back from a brief visit with his parents. Suddenly, a bolt of lightning ripped through the black sky. The thunderous peal shook the earth and threw the young man to the ground. Walled about with the terror and agony of sudden death, he cried out, *"Ich will ein Monch werden"*—I will become a monk.

Martin Luther took little thought that afternoon about changing the world. He merely wanted to save his own skin. But he was true to his vow, and on July 17, 1505, the massive door of the great Augustinian cloister in Erfurt closed behind Luther.

My illustration was interrupted by Michael, who began to laugh for no apparent reason. Then we realized he was watching Bob make clown faces at him from across the room.

Richard put his arm on the back of Crystal's chair and said, "I can imagine the sound of those huge gates as they closed behind the young seminarian. He must've felt as frightened as a raw recruit at boot camp."

I waited a few minutes for Jill and Crystal to return with the twins from the bathroom and continued my story undaunted.

There was no peace for this fiery young theologian. His spirit burned with a vengeance. He desired to know God. The outwardly serene life of a monk loomed as a constant paradox which mocked Luther's inner turmoil. He was consumed with remorse and bewilderment. The contentment and fulfillment that he knew must be within his reach eluded him.

Days of fasting and grief filled his waking moments. After one long session of anguish and tears, a brother came to him and burst with anger, "You are a fool! God is not angry with you. You are angry with God."

The Bible was his only solace. Luther said, "If you picture the Bible as a mighty tree and every word a little branch, I have shaken every one of these branches because I wanted to know what it was and what it meant." After ten years of ardent study and meditation, Martin's focus was fixed on Romans 1:17, "For therein is the righteousness of God revealed. . . . The just shall live by faith."

"The whole Scripture revealed a different countenance to me," Martin explained. God's mercy was given to man freely. As our flesh dies, the Spirit of life and love is born in us through Jesus Christ. Grace is not earned, but wonderfully and generously given as an act of love by God through the great sacrifice of Jesus.

Martin was set free of his anguish, fear, suffering, and grief. "This passage in Paul opened for me the gate of paradise. I felt I was born again."

But God was not finished with Martin Luther. Friar Johann Tetzel began selling indulgences at the city markets near Wittenberg where he was serving as parish priest. Daily confrontation with this blatant contradiction of Scripture enraged Luther. He knew that the assurances given when a person paid the price to buy a loved one from purgatory were false, and he feared for the salvation of his parishioners. He preached against indulgences and questioned them in public.

Crystal sat up in her chair, pulled her youngest daughter onto her lap. "What are indulgences? I was raised a Baptist and never understood that concept."

I told them that the assistant editor of *National Geographic,* Merle Severy, explains the medieval understanding of the indulgence: "Indulgences offered a popular palliative. Christ, mankind's Redeemer, and His saints had built up an infinite reservoir of merits, church doctrine declared. The Pope at his discretion could draw upon this treasure and award these credits to a sinner in return for a good work such as giving alms. A papal bull (or declaration) extended this so that the living could also procure indulgences for the dead."

Finally Luther could no longer tolerate the sale of the hateful indulgences. He defied the Church and the Holy Roman Empire by nailing his ninety-five theses on the church door in Wittenberg. Later, when Rome quizzed Luther at an inquisition held before Emperor Charles V at Worms, Luther said, "I cannot and will not recant." His act of defiance rocked the empire as well as the Church.

Luther risked everything, including his life, for what he knew to be true. God used him to change the face of the Church and Europe. Although it was a common practice for men to be martyred because of the smallest infraction of the law, God spared Luther's life and used him to reform and transform the world.

In the early morning hours when I had read the account of Luther, I was impressed with how one man or one woman, empowered by the Holy Spirit, can shake kingdoms and rock the sandy foundation of a religion that had existed for centuries. Yet without the work of God's grace, we can never change a single hair on our own head or the heads of the people who are dearest to us.

I had recounted the story of Luther's magnificent journey for Crystal and Richard and the rest of the family during our meal. As we started eating dessert, I commented, "The epitome of defiance of the free will God has given to man is manipulation. While we may instinctively know what would be best for our loved ones, we cannot use the inappropriate power of manipulation to work the changes that only God can perform."

"For years," Jill said in agreement, "I used every trick in the book to try to control Pat and make him into the man I wanted. I could see his shortcomings, and I could imagine how wonderful Pat would be if only he could hear what I was saying. My problem was that I didn't really understand that I could never change Pat.

"I payed lip service to the fact that Pat was a free agent, but I intended to do my part to be sure that he knew what great possibilities were out on the horizon, if only he would choose to do things my way." Jill wiped Michael's chocolate-covered hands and mouth while she finished her confession.

Richard had listened intently to the story of Luther's life. As the conversation had naturally flowed into a discussion of manipulation, he had continued to listen. Crystal, however, had withdrawn from the adult talk and started to playfully tease Sarah and Andrea.

Jill turned to her in an attempt to bring her back into the flow of the conversation. "On a popular television talk show recently," Jill said, "a psychologist was being interviewed. Her specialty is counseling divorced men and women. She said, 'You must realize that you do not have the power to change anyone. The problem with most marriages is that one or both of the partners go into the wedding day with a hidden agenda of how they will change their spouse once the nuptial knot is firmly tied. It will never work. The instant that a person imagines that you want him to change he will dig in his heels and determine that he will not succumb to any amount of pressure or harassment.

" 'I advise people who are considering marriage or remarriage to pick out someone who is as close to being the person they want as they can find and to decide that they will be able to live with the faults that are already apparent.' "

At this juncture in the conversation, Crystal stood up at the table and threw her napkin on top of her half-eaten banana pudding. Pointing her long, slender finger at Richard, she spoke with a calm voice, but anger was darting from her eyes. "How could you do this to me?" It was apparent that she was fighting back tears as she left the restaurant.

Richard was as stunned as the rest of us. He got up from his chair to follow her. "What did I do this time?" he said in honest confusion.

"Stay here with the girls; let me talk to her," Jill said, reaching over to place her hand on his. She gathered up Michael and quickly followed Crystal out of the restaurant. Stephen, Thomas, Andrea, and Sarah were delegated to the care of the older children for a few minutes, as Richard and I tried to figure out what had triggered Crystal's negative response.

"I'll never win," Richard said in disgust. He was embarrassed by Crystal's show of anger and emotion. I understood that his irritation was rooted in the fact that he had lost control of the situation. More than being embarrassed by Crystal, his loss of control frustrated Richard. It didn't surprise me that he said, "I don't want to talk anymore. It's apparent to everyone in the restaurant that I'm a failure as a husband. Crystal and I will never understand each other."

With an empathy that comes from having fared poorly when faced with the same frustrations in my own life, I said, "Wait a minute. Let's go back and analyze what happened. Women aren't the big mystery we've imagined, Richard. They are only different. Something happened between the two of you that triggered her outburst."

"No. There was nothing. I'd remember."

Reliving those famous masculine words, I almost chuckled out loud. Countless times, I'd reasoned with myself, *Jill exploded for*

*no reason. I've done nothing. If there had been something wrong,
I'd remember.*

Trying to wedge an opening through his discouragement, I
said, "Think about the events of this morning. What was said,
what happened? Go over it bit by bit with me. Perhaps I can help
you sort through the pieces."

"Same old thing. Crystal fixed my favorite breakfast, so I
knew something was up. Sure enough, by the time I was putting
jelly on my second biscuit, she began her play. First, she took my
hand and said in a real sweet voice that she had talked with Jill
yesterday. Then she suggested, ever so nicely, that I should make
an appointment with you.

"I had already made up my mind to see you this morning, but
when I realized that she was trying to con me into it, I said
something about wanting to go fishing instead of seeing you after
church.

"She brought it up again while we were dressing. She was
sitting on the edge of the bed and putting on her stockings. The
fact that she is most appealing during that time almost softened
me, but I was able to resist.

"When Crystal snuggled up beside me in the car on our way
to church, I knew that I had no resistance left for her final assault.
Of course, I enjoyed the full benefits of her persuasive powers
before I let her know that I'd talk with you. What did I do wrong?
Sure, I resisted seeing you, but I agreed in the end."

Remembering the dinner conversation, I knew why Crystal
had become angry and defensive. "Crystal felt this luncheon was
a setup to correct her. She wrongly assumed that you'd talked
with me about her impressive performance this morning. She had
used those wifely, manipulative manuevers to persuade you to
have a talk with me. When the Holy Spirit directed our conversation to manipulation, she became convicted."

"Pat, I don't understand her. I don't think I ever will."

"My concern is that you will never try to understand her.
Someday, you'll see that keeping your marriage exciting and
fascinating is a blessing from God. Understanding Crystal is far
more rewarding than any satisfaction you can achieve from a

promotion at the office. Richard, have you ever really *tried* to see her side of the situation?''

"How could I? What's the use? Crystal doesn't think like a man. She's totally illogical. Nothing she does makes sense. It's like she's a catamaran in the middle of a storm without any rudder.''

"Do you realize that you've just exposed three basic problems women wrestle with in their relationships to their husbands? First, men don't understand their wives. Second, most men don't try to understand their partners because women aren't built like men—they are totally illogical. And third, almost all men believe that women are inferior to them because a woman's thinking processes are different.''

"That sums up my feelings exactly,'' Richard said, rather proud of our superior, manly logic.

Hating to burst his inflated-ego bubble, I said, "You have just admitted that you have some serious sin areas in your life.'' Richard's mouth hung open, but I didn't give him an opportunity to say anything. Instead I continued.

"The first thing you need to give Crystal is your understanding. I can understand your frustration with what has happened this afternoon because I've been in your place. I've been the husband who couldn't comprehend his wife's needs or anger. When I gave Jill what she wanted, she only found ten other areas to complain about. I know where you are coming from because I've been there.

"You have to understand Crystal from a different vantage point. The ivory tower approach won't work with her. You can't look down from the lofty perspective of having lived through the conflict and come out victorious. You must understand women differently. The 1828 Noah Webster's dictionary defines understanding as 'the faculty of the human mind by which it . . . comprehends the ideas which others express and intend to communicate.' ''

I shared what Dennis and Barbara Rainey expressed in their book, *Building Your Mate's Self-Esteem:* "Understanding, then is not just a transference of information, but an empathy for the other person based on what was shared or communicated.''

"Women are continually trying to share the details of their lives with us," I said. Richard rolled his eyes up and shook his head in agreement. "We see no point in that exhausting exercise. But there is a logical explanation to their behavior. By putting details to the facts, women are seeking to comprehend the context of our lives. Context helps explain behavior and attitudes.

"Everyone knows the Indian proverb that says you can't know a man until you have walked a mile in his moccasins. We must start to understand our wives. Proverbs 24:3 (NAS) says, 'By wisdom a house is built, and by understanding it is established.'

"The next time Crystal expresses a concern about her hair or her cooking or your marriage, ask her if she believes that you understand what she is saying. Listen to her with a sympathetic ear. Practice looking into her eyes and hearing the words she is saying. Look beyond her response to the cause of that response. What pressures in the past have shaped her attitude? What has occurred during the day to crush her spirit and produce the hurt?

"When we came to the crisis time in our marriage, I sensed that our relationship would flourish and grow if I treated Jill with discernment and dug underneath the surface to the depths of her mind and soul.

"Charles Swindoll has said that a marriage is established on understanding. 'When husbands respond to wives with a high degree of insight and sensitivity, marriages can be corrected and put in order. When we use wisdom it is no longer necessary to take conflicts and irritation personally, but we can see them from God's vantage point as being either good or essential for our further growth.'

"As a man you feel you don't have to understand your wife because she isn't logical. There are two reasons that women appear to be illogical to men. The first reason is because women operate from a different—though not inferior—perspective. Men are taught to be materialistic. Their goals are built around a good job and providing an adequate living for their families.

"A woman's primary concern is with the relationships in her

life. She intuitively comprehends that if the relationships are out of kilter, her whole life will be tilted.

"The second reason women appear illogical is because they operate from an intuitive perspective. Their logic stems from what they 'know' through their intuition.

"When Sarah said to Abraham, 'Get that woman (Hagar) and her son (Ishmael) out of my house,' God agreed with Sarah and told Abraham to do what Sarah said. Abraham loved his son Ishmael, who was approximately fourteen years old. He didn't want to drive him away from their home, but Sarah knew intuitively that they were living in an impossible situation, and God agreed.

"We tend to argue with our wives when they say, 'I don't think you should do that.'

" 'Why not?' we ask.

" 'I don't know. I just don't think it's a good idea.'

" 'Give me one good reason why it's not a good idea.'

" 'Because I don't feel right about it.'

" 'Give me one good reason why it's not a good idea.'

" 'I did.'

" 'No, you didn't.'

" 'Yes, I did. I said that I don't feel right about it.' "

Richard exploded in laughter, "Crystal and I had that same conversation last night. I wanted to go to the mountains on our vacation. Some business friends have a cottage there, and they have offered to lend it to us for two weeks in the summer.

"Crystal wanted to veto the whole trip until I put my foot down. I told her that if she could come up with one good, logical reason, the trip would be cancelled. But all she would say was, 'I don't feel right about it.' "

"What was the feeling you had when the argument was over?"

"I felt that it was a good thing that Crystal had me or she would be like a lost puppy wandering around chasing her tail."

"In other words, you feel that because Crystal appears illogical in her thinking, she is inferior."

"That's for sure."

"But the Bible plainly teaches that God looks on Crystal as

equal to you. Different in personality—yes. But she's not inferior. I've known for a long time now that Sarah wasn't the only
wife who could hear from God for her husband. God can speak
clearly to a husband through his wife.''

"Remember that you're dealing with a person who is intuitive
and who prizes her relationships above almost everything else. If
you feel that she is not quite up to your par, she will sense that,
and it will drive a wedge of discouragement and rebellion between you.''

As Pat talked with Richard, I whisked up Michael and followed Crystal back to their car. When Crystal saw me, she broke
down and started to cry. "How could Richard do that to me? I
thought you and Pat were going to help me. But there you all
were ganging up on me until I couldn't take it another minute.
I'm sorry I exploded, but it wasn't fair.''

"Crystal, what are you talking about?'' I asked as we started
to walk around the parking lot, which was lined with sidewalks,
trees, and park benches. Michael followed behind, happily picking up fallen acorns and throwing them into the cracks of the
sidewalk.

"All that business about manipulation. Richard told you about
what I did this morning to get him to see Pat. I used every trick
I could think of from sex to biscuits. I could see Pat and Richard
conspiring against me but when you joined them, I couldn't take
it.''

"Wait a minute. Richard did not talk with Pat this morning. I
overheard the conversation they had at the van, and they said
nothing about you. In fact, all they talked about was going out to
lunch. They didn't even have time to discuss the football game,''
I said, adding the convincing clincher.

"Crystal, the Holy Spirit directed our conversation—not Richard. The fact that you responded with such conviction tells me
that He was right on target.''

"I guess we've found another problem area in my life,'' Crystal mumbled. Her head was down as she kicked an imaginary
rock, but I could see that she was smiling. "I do tend to manipulate Richard. Is that really wrong?''

"Yes, but people don't often understand the depth of the sin they commit. Jesus said, 'Which of you by being anxious can add a single cubit to his life's span?' While God refuses to violate the free will of His creation, we glibly set out to change and rearrange.

"Manipulation is setting up circumstances in order to change another person. At the onset of Pat's and my relationship, I did two things. The first one was right; I asked my mother to pray. She is a fierce prayer warrior, and there was no way that Pat had a chance once she believed that God wanted us together.

"The other thing I did, however, set a precedent for the years that followed. I arranged situations to make Pat notice me. This wasn't like me. However, even when we met, I had gone to a church where I knew he was speaking. I only went to meet him. I'd never done that kind of thing. After he had spoken, I got into a line where he was signing autographs for the young boys in the audience.

"During our courtship, it was fun and exciting to see if I could get his attention—a playful, seemingly harmless game. Yet patterns were being set which would be acted out with the consequence of causing years of heartbreak and frustration for both of us.

"Martin Luther didn't set out to change the world, but God had ordained him as the reformer, the innovator. God had ordained that Pat and I become one, but for years I wasn't satisfied to let God do His miracles of change. Once we were married, I set out to change Pat. Manipulation became a full-time job, but it never did and never will reap lasting results," I said as I reached down to take Michael's hand.

Crystal turned around. "Let's go back into the restaurant. I need to rearrange my face and makeup. Then I owe Richard and Pat an apology."

By the time we rejoined Pat and Richard at the table, the children—who had been unusually patient—were quickly approaching the restless stage. Jim had retrieved a puzzle book from the van for them to draw in. But as the minutes dragged on, they had grown tired of their book activities. Bob was conducting an exciting *scientific* experiment with the Sweet 'n Low. While I helped clean up their laboratory, Pat led Richard and Crystal in a short, to-the-point prayer of repentance and forgiveness.

By now the restaurant was empty, except for our families. Even the waitresses were sitting in an out-of-the-way corner facing the other direction. Pat's prayer was appropriate even under those unusual circumstances.

When the whole crew left, I heard the cashier sing an exceptionally relieved, "Good-bye, all."

I winked at Pat, "I think we're leaving right on time."

Chapter Six

Was There Life Before the Van?

When the girls come home from school in the afternoon, I spend time with each of them and we are able to do "girl-type projects." Andrea takes art lessons. Sarah has ballet and swimming. Karyn is involved in gymnastics and piano. Part of our time together is spent in the van, traveling from one class to another. I'm thankful for the spaciousness of a van and can't imagine trying to transport all of our crew without one.

During the years I was totally miserable in our marriage, I often toyed with the idea of becoming a full-time Christian musician. At the darkest ebb of my despair, I cut a record. Long after the last recording session, I continued to spend hours at the studio. I was a backup singer and violinist for several Christian records. I even did a few commercials.

Being involved in Christian music at this time in Church history is exciting. Styles in tempo and rhythm are being developed now which are producing a high-quality, pleasing sound. Gone is the scratchy record with the twanging guitar and honky-tonk piano. Orchestration and arrangements which were barely dreamed of twenty-five years ago are now the norm in the Christian music world.

When you compare driving almost fifty miles each day to transport children, to the excitement of a recording contract and career in the skyrocketing field of Christian music, there seems to be few points to stack in the traffic-hustling column.

I could more than understand Crystal's enthusiasm when she showed up one afternoon with a catalog from a local college. Her girls were going home with their grandmother from school, and she had the afternoon free. "I've decided that a part-time job at the church isn't enough for me. I need a career."

"Have you talked this over with Richard?" I asked, trying to appear nonchalant while I browsed through the schedule of classes.

"Don't tell me you disapprove of my taking a few classes to improve myself, too."

"Wait a minute. Why the defensiveness? First of all, you didn't say you were going to take a few classes. You said you needed a career."

"Well, what's wrong with that?" Four-year-old Michael had come to me and held his hands out for me to pick him up. He had a ladybug in his fist. We admired the tiny spotted wonder as Crystal continued. "The girls are in school all day. I have time on my hands. We don't plan on having any more children. Our home isn't the ideal environment for children anyway. We can't even decide on the color to paint the walls in the living room without a battle that rivals the Korean conflict. I don't think that's the kind of home life children need."

"You're right, and there is nothing wrong with a career if Richard agrees, and you're home in the afternoons when school lets out."

"He's old-fashioned. He doesn't even want me to work part-time at the church. He thinks I should let him earn all the money and sit around the rest of my life twiddling my thumbs."

"Is a career what you really want?"

"I refuse to end up like most women. Face it, Jill, I'm the

product of a different generation. And to be honest, I refuse to end up like you. I don't think you even remember what life was like before you became a van jockey.''

"Oh, yes, I remember."

"Why did you do it?" Crystal asked me with a sincerity which replaced the biting sarcasm that had gripped her tone of voice during our entire conversation.

"Why did I do what?" I asked as I picked up my carryall and keys to the van. "Come with me to get the children from school. We'll talk on the way. Get your jacket and hop in the van, Michael."

"Why did you give up a promising recording career to haul children from one end of Orlando, Florida, to another? Jill, your life is a complete waste."

By now we had peeled off into the main stream of traffic on the interstate. "Crystal, I want you to notice what happens when I drive up to the school to pick up the kids. There will be six marvelous smiles waiting for me. Bob, Stephen, and Thomas have basketball practice after school, so they will kiss me hello and drop off their books. Karyn, Andrea, and Sarah will get into the van and chatter all the way home about new discoveries and exciting wonders of the day.

"I wouldn't give up those joys for enough money to buy all the Oriental rugs in China. One smile gives me more satisfaction than a million records that I might sell. A slobbery kiss from a four-year-old full of peanut butter and jelly replaces any fame I could ever obtain. You're a mother. You know that."

Crystal smiled and nodded her head in agreement. Perhaps as an unconscious, symbolic gesture, she put the college catalog into her purse under the seat.

I swung the van up to the front of the school and six faces beamed at my arrival. "They are my career," I said, as I reached over to unlock the back double doors to let in the girls.

"Now I'm confused," Crystal said as she admired a picture that Andrea, our resident artist, had drawn during class. "I thought you'd be pleased because I'd started to look at the next step of ANOINT. Remember, *Notice Your Needs*. I thought about this for a week, and I decided that having a career would meet my needs.''

"I think you missed the point. The needs that Pat was talking about were those deep desires and longings which are put in your spirit by God—not by the current fashion of the age,'' I said. After a brief commercial break about the wonders of the seat belt from Sarah, I pulled away from the school parking lot. "What are the deep yearnings of your heart?''

"Oh,'' Crystal said. Karyn, Andrea, and Sarah chatted with me about Karyn's new teacher and how beautiful she was. Crystal was quiet. She joined in our conversation to smile and nod, but it was apparent her thoughts were no longer with us. A chord had been struck inside her heart. I couldn't tell whether that chord produced a joy so moving that she was having to contain it with stillness, or a pain too deep to share with anyone.

After we had dropped Karyn off at gymnastics practice, I turned the van toward home. Crystal looked out the window. When I pulled up into the driveway, she opened the door and helped Michael get out. "I won't go inside,'' she said. "But could we meet somewhere for lunch tomorrow?''

"Sure. Which hamburger haven do you want to go to?''

"What about Wendy's on Highway 17-92 at noon?''

The next day Michael and I were early, so we sat out under the trees as we waited for Crystal. I sat on the curb while Michael inspected an anthill in the grass. I wondered if the emotions in Crystal which had been churned up yesterday had settled. Her compact pulled into the space beside our van, and we went into the restaurant to get our hamburgers.

Finding a table next to the window, we faced the large oak tree that Michael and I had been sitting under. Spanish moss swayed lazily in the breeze. I wasn't anxious to initiate the conversation. I felt that Crystal needed freedom to tell me her thoughts or to keep them private.

"I told Richard that I'm not going to go back to school after all. I don't need a degree to fulfill the deep needs of my heart,'' Crystal said as she took her salad, hamburger, and iced tea off her tray and placed the tray on another table. I didn't comment but handed Michael a napkin so he could wipe the mayonnaise off his cheek.

"Jill, I was absolutely astounded by what you shared yesterday. I never imagined that the deep needs of my heart have been placed there by God. Now that I think about it, it seems elementary that He would be the Author of those things, but I'd always considered them selfish and tried to cover them up.

"When I saw that God could be the One who had placed them within me and had initiated them, I spent yesterday afternoon writing. I did a lot of rewriting, too. Finally, I'd scaled my needs down to several basic things.

"I don't want this to sound religious, but I really need to have a deeper relationship with Jesus. I look at people I admire and they all have an intimate friendship with the Lord. There is such a stirring inside of me for that.

"Last month after I agreed to teach the five-year-old Sunday school class at the church, I almost panicked. I could gloss over those forty-five minutes each Sunday, but I'm not like that. I started reading my Bible for the first time. I have a simple plan, four chapters a day, Monday through Saturday. I decided to begin in the Gospels. I'm almost finished with John now.

"My heart aches to be able to know Jesus like a friend. Is there something that you and Pat do that will help me in getting to know Jesus?" Crystal asked while taking a bite of her salad.

"A deep longing to know God is the first step we take in having a relationship with Him. Andrew Murray in his classic book, *Absolute Surrender,* said that we are to cast ourselves at the feet of Jesus, and then trust Him. We cannot worry ourselves with trying to understand all about Him, but rest in the living faith that Christ will come into us with the power of His death and the power of His life.

"Pat and I have found that there are three basic steps we need to heed in order to keep our relationship with the Lord strong and growing. They aren't complicated, but they are extremely necessary. Over the years, I've seen that the people who are constantly growing in their relationship with the Lord have developed these essentials into their life's disciplines.

"The first thing you should do is read the Scriptures every day. I'm excited to hear that you're doing that already. You also need to develop a prayer life. We complicate prayer, but I like the definition Billy Graham gave for prayer years ago: 'Prayer is the deep yearning of the heart directed toward God.' Each day should begin and end with a quiet time of prayer. The position of our bodies isn't as important as the longing of our hearts.

"With the advent of Christian television, the third basic step to growth can't be ignored. It is fellowship with other Christians. The Church is full of hypocrites and phonies, but she is the organism God has chosen as His instrument on earth. We need each other."

Crystal looked as though she were literally drinking in my suggestions. I continued, "I don't mean to sound simplistic but if you will do these things while desiring to know God, there will be growth in your life."

The openness which I began to see in Crystal's face was encouraging. She slowly turned her iced-tea glass between her hands as though in deep thought and remarked, "I also need to know that Richard loves me. He always says, 'Of course, I love you. I married you, didn't I?' I guess that should be enough, but it's not for me.

"My last need will sound strange to everybody. I've never even dared to verbalize it before last night because it seemed odd that anyone would have a deep need like this. I mulled it over and over yesterday afternoon. I finally concluded that it wasn't merely a freaky quirk but a seed that God has put within me.

"Jill, please don't laugh, but I'd like to take care of a pre-school child during the day. I have always had a burden for young, single mothers who have children and have to work to support them. I'd like to take one child into our home and love him.

"I told you about the terrible ordeal my mother went through when I was a teenager. Even though it may seem as though that would be the most horrible time for me, my mother and father shielded me a lot from the torment of those years. There was a bad time for me, however, when I was about two or three years old.

"Daddy had gotten sick—not alcoholism—he had contracted an unknown virus. He was recently out of the service and his insurance paid his hospital and doctor bills, but we had nothing to live on. Mother had to work for the months that he was in the hospital and then for another year while he was recuperating and they were catching up with their finances.

"Mother put me in a day-care center. I guess for some children that would be great, but it was a torture chamber for me. I was painfully shy and immature for my age. The children sensed my awkwardness. None of them liked me. They hurt me, spit on me, hit me, and bit me. I still have nightmares about having to go back there.

"I told Richard about this need last night. Jill, he said that he'd love for me to take care of a child. He's even willing to get a crib or a bed for the spare room. He was excited and making plans to help me.

"When my children were babies, I would have never thought that I would be happy taking care of someone else's baby. But for now, I know that it's the right thing for us—for me. As you know, I've been working at the church two mornings a week. I'm going to reduce that to one day.

"I can't tell you how happy I am at this moment. I checked the morning papers and I have an interview with a mother this afternoon after she comes home from work. She's the lady who lives in the corner house as you turn into our neighborhood. She's a widow whose husband died of cancer last year. She needs to work a couple of days a week because she has three other children who are in school. Her husband didn't leave enough insurance to cover all their expenses. She can't bear to sell their home and tear the other children away from their friends and school routines."

Crystal's grin was contagious. "Isn't that perfect?" she squealed.

I was genuinely happy for Crystal, but it was hard to show. At that precise moment, Michael lifted the plastic lid from his paper cup and spilled water all over the front of his coveralls.

When Pat called that afternoon, I was able to tell him about Crystal's good news with the enthusiasm I had lacked in the restaurant. "Maybe that's why Richard called me this afternoon," Pat commented. "I haven't had time to return his call but I will as soon as I hang up.

"You know, Jill, I'm amazed at the wisdom and diversity of God," Pat said. "We are all completely different. There are those basic hungers to know God and to be loved. But beyond that, each of us has a burning desire that's been shaped by circumstances and nurtured by the Holy Spirit that is as unique as each individual.

"I've never realized more than I do now that we are fearfully and wonderfully made."

Chapter Seven

Notice Your Need

After I hung up from the conversation with Jill, my secretary came into my office with several important messages. She always holds my calls and appointments when I'm talking with Jill or the children.

It was several hours before I could take another break. While I'd not forgotten to call Richard back, there had not been a minute to spare, and now the day was almost over. When I dialed the number, they told me that he had already left his office for home.

I glanced at my watch and realized that the afternoon had slipped away, and it was time for me to pick up the boys from school. Their basketball practice would be over and they would be waiting by the time I reached them.

Picking up my briefcase, I hurried out of the office. As I traveled in the stop-and-start, late-afternoon traffic, I prayed for Crystal and Richard. Jill had told me about the three needs that Crystal had shared. "Pat," Jill had commented to me, "there wasn't much I could say to Crystal when she told me she needed assurance of Richard's love. Do you think that we need to talk to them together again?''

Of course, Jill and I weren't surprised that needing Richard's love was at the top of Crystal's list. I also had a sneaky suspicion that if Richard were honest he would list needing Crystal's love as a deep need that he had.

Because we are in our vehicles so much of the time, Jill and I found that car phones have become essential for us to keep up with each other. I called her as I traveled toward the boys' school. Jill was preparing stir-fried chicken for supper. I could hear her sniffling as she chopped the onions while we talked.

"I was going over your talk with Crystal in my mind. If Richard is honest with me, what do you think that one of his top needs will be?" I asked.

Jill laughed. She had already guessed where my mind was headed. "That's easy. He has a need for Crystal's love."

"Right." I said, reassured that we were heading in the right direction.

"But, Pat, you and I know that Crystal and Richard will be talking about two entirely different things."

"That's right. Crystal will be talking about romance and Richard will be talking about sex. How are we going to bridge that gap in their minds?"

"I don't know, babe," Jill said, with a question in her voice. "I don't think a simple answer will suffice for them. Men and women are radically different when they think about these subjects."

"It may take several times together over the course of months for them to understand the diverse differences in their opinions," I said, agreeing with her.

"That's why I said we should talk with them together. You explain and I'll pray," Jill said.

By this time, I'd arrived at school. Thomas, Stephen, and Bob were standing together on the sidewalk with their gym bags in hand. As they jumped into the car, it was suddenly filled with laughing, poking, wiggles, and giggles. All thoughts of the difference between romantic love and sex were replaced with the "elementary-school joke of the day." I made another stop to pick up Jim from his basketball practice, and we were on our way home.

The dinner Jill had prepared smelled wonderful. Sarah and Andrea had set the table, and Karyn was helping her mother put the salad in place. All of the Williams' men headed for the kitchen, eager to help with the last-minute details. We hoped that any assistance we gave would speed up the process of being able to eat.

Sarah, the family hostess, shooed us out of the kitchen into the bathroom to wash our hands, and by the time we were finished, the candles were lit and the food was ready to eat. After the blessing and a time of talking with the children, Jill said in a playful voice, "Richard called. He sounded pretty anxious. Said he really needs to talk with you. The ball is in your court, Williams."

Dr. James Dobson said on a recent radio program that the true goal of every person is intimacy. Almost all women have a better understanding of intimacy than most men. Women will give sexual favors in order to obtain intimacy, but a man will feign intimacy in order to get sex.

Knowing the marked difference between a man's and woman's idea of love and intimacy, I knew that Crystal and Richard had an uphill climb. Charles Swindoll has written, "There is an incredible difference between the sexual appetite of a man and the sexual appetite of a woman."

Recognizing those differences, Dr. Dobson wrote in, *What Wives Wish Their Husbands Knew About Women* (Tyndale, 1983):

> First, men are primarily excited by *visual* stimulation. They are turned on by feminine nudity or peek-a-boo glimpses of semi-nudity. . . . Women, by contrast, are much less visually oriented than men. Sure they are interested in attractive masculine bodies, but the physiological mechanism of sex is not triggered typically by what they see; women are stimulated primarily by the sense of touch. Thus, we encounter the first source of disagreement in the bedroom: he wants her to appear unclothed in a lighted room, and she wants him to caress her in the dark.
>
> Second (and much more important), men are not very dis-

criminating in regard to the person living within an exciting body. A man can walk down a street and be stimulated by a scantily clad female who shimmies past him, even though he knows nothing about her personality or values or mental capabilities. He is attracted by her body itself. Likewise, he can become almost as excited over a photograph of an unknown nude model as he can in a face-to-face encounter with someone he loves. In essence, the sheer biological power of sexual desire in a male is largely focused on the physical body of an attractive female. Hence, there is some validity to the complaint by women that they have been used as "sex objects" by men. This explains why female prostitutes outnumber males by a wide margin and why few women try to "rape" men. It explains why a roomful of toothless old men can get a charge from watching a burlesque dancer "take it all off." It reflects the fact that masculine self-esteem is more motivated by a desire to "conquer" a woman than in becoming the object of her romantic love. These are not very flattering characteristics of male sexuality, but they are well documented in the professional literature. All of these factors stem from a basic difference in sexual appetites of males and females.

Women are much more discriminating in their sexual interests. They less commonly become excited by observing a good-looking charmer, or by the photograph of a hairy model; rather, their desire is usually focused on a *particular* individual whom they respect or admire. A woman is stimulated by the romantic aura which surrounds her man, and by his character and personality. She yields to the man who appeals to her emotionally as well as physically. Obviously, there are exceptions to these characteristic desires, but the fact remains, sex for men is a more physical thing; sex for women is a deeply emotional experience.

Crystal and Richard fit the descriptive pattern described by Dr. Dobson. Crystal is open but manipulative. Richard seemed to be strong, self-made, and the ultimate macho man.

The phone rang, interrupting my thoughts. "Why don't you answer it, Pat? I'm sure it's for you," Jill said, trying not to laugh at my dilemma. As she guessed, it was Richard.

"I need to spend some time with Jim and help him with a homework project," Jill informed me, grinning her wonderful smile. "You could meet with him right after the children are in bed, if you have nothing else planned and that's convenient for him."

I smiled and made a seven o'clock appointment.

When Richard arrived at the house, Jim's science project was spread all over the living room and dining room table. We decided to talk at the coffee shop down the road.

"Crystal's really happy about what happened yesterday. She met with the lady who has the baby, and she's going to be keeping her three days a week. I don't think that I've ever seen such a sudden change in anyone. I never even knew that Crystal wanted to keep a child before. I can't tell you how much you and Jill are helping her."

"What about you?" I asked as we reached the coffee shop.

"Hey, I'm not sure I have any real needs. My job is going good. Our house has been my big project for the last two years and that's almost under control. There'll always be some repairs with a home like ours, but I can see light at the end of the tunnel now."

Richard and Crystal had purchased a large home at the end of our street. It had once been a beautiful showplace, but a family of three bachelor men, all brothers, with four dogs had rented it and lived there for seven years. When the brothers moved, the house had been almost completely destroyed. During the years the men had lived there, the owner had died. The family had allowed the brothers to stay in the house as long as they paid the rent. When they moved out, however, it became part of an estate sale. Richard and Crystal had purchased it for just a little more than the price of the back taxes.

These two young people had taken on the project of cleaning and repairing their new home like two excited beavers. Once they had gotten into the project, they found that the major headaches of almost all older houses were absent. In fact, the plumbing and electrical wiring had been completely replaced. When the condemned carpets were ripped up, they found magnificent oak floors.

With a minimal amount of money, a maximum amount of

germ warfare, and enough hard labor to kill an elephant, they had transformed the neighborhood eyesore into a clean, livable home. Everyone in our neighborhood, including Richard, was proud of the amount of work that had been accomplished in the house during the two years.

After we had ordered some herb tea, Richard commented, "There is one thing, though. If I could only get Crystal to enjoy sex, I would be a totally happy man."

"Did Crystal tell you about her list of needs?" I asked Richard.

"Yeah, and I guess that's why I wanted to meet with you. I don't understand. She wants me to give her assurance that I love her. Pat, I try to be the best lover I can. Even if I'm dead tired, we have sex almost every day.

"The weird part is that Crystal usually doesn't want to have sex. When we get in bed and I try to make advances to her, she will literally push my hands away and sometimes even tell me to leave her alone. I have no idea what she wants from me." Richard sighed and stared at his tea.

"First, let me assure you that I understand your confusion. It will be impossible to cover everything about this subject tonight. We can scratch the surface—not perform major surgery. Later, we'll be able to go deeper into this vital part of your life. There is probably no other area in marriage where men and women talk two entirely different languages than in the area of romantic love.

"When Susan says she wants love, George's mind automatically takes a flying leap between the sheets. At the same time, if George says, 'I love you, dear,' Susan envisions fifty years of walking hand in hand down a long, tree-lined, moss-laden country road with violins playing softly in the background."

Richard scratched his head, "Pat, I don't have the slightest idea what you're talking about."

"Hasn't Crystal ever told you that she would much rather hold your hand than have you make overt sexual advances to her?"

"Of course, she has, but I don't believe her. It's only part of the game women are taught to play. You know—hard to get."

"Richard, I know your confusion, but believe me when I tell

you that Crystal is absolutely serious when she says she would rather have you hold her hand than make a sexual advance."

"That's crazy. We're married. The need for all that hand-holding business went out the window on our wedding night."

"Maybe for you, but not for her."

"Are you saying that Crystal doesn't want to have sex? I've figured that was the case for a long time now. In fact, I've told her that there is something wrong with her. Maybe she should go see a doctor."

"Jill and I were talking about this very thing the other night. She explained to me that for a woman, the romantic part of marriage is like closing the door to the outside world. There's the frantic pace of schedules, meetings, children, jobs. The washing machine vomits, the commode explodes—all on the day the dog has diarrhea and your mother is coming for a week's visit. The romantic part of love allows a man to wrap his wife in a protective shield which takes her away from the pressure and allows her to become a woman again. Once the pressure is totally off, then she can respond in a sexual way."

Richard still looked puzzled. "A lot of women are saying they don't want to be thought of as a sex object. I've figured that was some feminist propaganda. Maybe they're saying what you've been saying."

"Perhaps. Women want romance without the pressure of performance. They desire that each encounter with their husband be fresh and spontaneous. That's impossible, of course, but we can at least try."

"Pat, be honest. Don't you think that's stupid?"

"I did a few years ago. But I've seen that romance works for Jill and for me. When I reinstated a romantic love into our marriage, it was a giant step toward healing our relationship.

"Jill and I have come to understand that there are six steps which will help to keep a marriage strong and growing. Think about them. Maybe they could be of benefit to your marriage.

"First, *Holiness and Godliness*—God should be at the center of your relationship. In talking with hundreds of Christian couples, all have asserted that God used circumstances to bring them together.

"Richard, remember when you first met Crystal. Were there supernatural events that led you to meet?"

"There sure were," Richard said. "I wasn't going to church that morning but to the beach. It rained. Crystal was visiting a friend in the Sunday school class. I was dating someone else and didn't even notice her, but she was impressed by a comment I made. She came up to me after class to ask me more details. I didn't have time to answer her question so I got her phone number and called her that afternoon. All along the way, I can point to drastic turning points, where God intervened to guide and direct our lives," Richard agreed.

"Your goal in marriage must be to make His will your highest aim," I said. "This will lead you to read your Bible daily, pray together, become active in church, and use the gifts God has given you. As a natural consequence, you will rear your children in the fear of the Lord, drawing behavioral standards from God's Word.

"Second, *Romantic Love*—Much is written about *agape* love—that is, the God-kind-of-love which transcends all sin and guilt and loves regardless of the impossibilities. *Agape* love is vital, but God also instituted romance. The greatest love stories in all history are found in the Bible: Ruth and Boaz, David and Bathsheba, Jacob and Rachel, Isaac and Rebekah.

"George Leonard said, 'We can orbit the earth, we can touch the moon, but this society has not devised a way for two people to live together in harmony for seven straight days without wanting to strangle each other.''

I told Richard that H. Norman Wright recently wrote in *Understanding The Men in Your Life*, "Men and women define love differently. All too often men confuse love with sex. For the most part they have a limited perspective on love. It is too narrow. It needs to be broadened and it can be. Men have a lot to learn from a woman's perspective. The problem is they do not want to admit this fact! It's a threat."

In her advice column, Ann Landers published a letter from a

man who was in torment because he feared that the woman he loved was deprived because a physical condition kept him from completing the sex act.

Mrs. Landers received a letter from a woman in Oregon who wrote in response to his letter:

> That man is totally ignorant of the working of the female mind and heart. If you were to ask 100 women how they feel about sexual intercourse, I'll bet 98 of them would say, "Just hold me close and be tender. Forget the rest." If you don't believe it, why not take a poll? People tell you things they would never tell anyone else.

Mrs. Landers asked women to respond. She phrased the question, "Would you be content to be held close and treated tenderly and forget about 'the act?' Answer YES or NO and please add one line: I am over or under forty years of age."

The mailrooms were flooded. The letter had struck a nerve. Over 100,000 women responded. As a result 72 percent of the women responded with YES, they would be content just to be held close and treated tenderly. Of those 72 percent, 40 percent were under forty.

"Women," Wright wrote, "have a fuller range for love. Love to a woman involves time spent together with significant interchange. It involves personal concern for one another and empathy. I have seen men who are willing to learn new ways of expressing love to their wives. It takes time and commitment and willingness to admit there is more to learn. Remember the point: It often takes a crisis for a man to be willing to change! A crisis occurs when a person's equilibrium is upset."

"Never stop saying 'I love you' to Crystal. A gentle squeeze of the hand, an unexpected note with endearing sentiments, a mischievous wink, surprise gifts, a dinner date once a week. In 1 Corinthians 7:3–5, Paul told the husband and wife that God commands us to meet one another's sexual needs. Simple things will keep your relationship sweet and special. That's all Crystal is asking for when she wants romance.

"Third, *Tenderness*—When asked about the abundant success of his television show, Bill Cosby said, 'This show says something very, very important. People are starved to see the love of husband and wife. They're starved to see genuine respect children have for their parents and parents for their children. If you give people something that addresses their problems and their concerns behaviorally, it doesn't make any difference what color the people are.'

"Paul instructed the Ephesians, 'Be ye kind one to another.' This applies to husbands and wives pitching in with chores and child care. There are many things we husbands can do to help our wives, but the physical tasks we perform are not nearly as important to them as our attitudes.

"Fourth, *Courtesy*—Being rude and inconsiderate embarrasses and drives people apart. 'Please,' 'Thank you,' 'I'm sorry' are words which are like keys. They can unlock the heart of almost everyone. With the kids, we laughingly call them 'magic' words, but they really can work wonders. Husbands and wives must be polite to one another.

"People in public life are observed carefully by the media. Not long ago I listened to a program on which two reporters discussed an aspiring presidential candidate. These were men who had traveled with him during previous campaigns. Both men stated that the candidate was generally not liked among the press corps. 'He has the personality of a president. He has the style of a great leader. He has the charisma and flair which put men in history, but those who follow him closely say there is a depth which is missing.'

"One newsman said that he and his colleagues had discussed the candidate's presidential mystique many times long into the night, and they tried to put a finger on the missing element within his character. 'Over and over again it was agreed that, generally, we do not approve of him because he is rude to his wife.

" 'I know that sounds puritanical,' confessed the reporter, 'but when a man appears that inconsiderate and that impolite to his life's partner, it says something about the inner person.'

"Fifth, *Understanding*—A man says, 'I think. . . .' A woman says, 'I feel. . . .' We must become sensitive to each other's strengths and weaknesses, likes and dislikes, virtues and failings. Each temperament is different. Listening and caring reassures Crystal of your unconditional love.

"As her husband you should understand and appreciate the differences in her. As you seek to enhance the variety she brings to your life, you will become a richer, more vital person.

"Sixth, *Loyalty*—A husband and wife should speak well of each other. Jill and I have made it a practice, especially in public, to always talk about the strong points we see in each other. We build each other up by being positive. Negative comments and observations are destructive. It's embarrassing for a couple to discuss their faults and failings outside the home."

"I realize that those things are important for Crystal, and I think I can see that perhaps they would help me, too," Richard confessed. "Though I have to tell you it still doesn't make sense to me. I started by saying I wish Crystal were more responsive to me in bed and you've given me the Boy Scout Code of Ethics. Be kind. Be loyal. . . ."

I couldn't help but laugh at him as he wrinkled up his nose. "Hey, Bro, it may never make sense," I said, "but I can almost guarantee you that if you want a better sex life, you need to romance Crystal the way you did when you were dating. And being considerate is a large part of romance.

"We men come in from a hard day at work. We growl at our wives, complain about the dinner, bark at the children, take a nap, watch TV, throw our clothes on the floor. Then we hop in bed and expect the little woman to become the love goddess of every man's dreams."

Thinking that our conversation was over, I was getting ready to leave. Yet I could tell that Richard had sunk into his own thoughts. I waited for him to speak.

In a few minutes, he said, "There is something I need to talk about." Richard spoke in a tone which barely reached a whisper. I strained to hear. "Pat, there is an area that few people detect in Crystal's life. At times she's like two different people. I'm not talking about a double personality or anything that drastic, but there is a side of Crystal that she only allows me to see. Crystal refuses to have anyone, and especially me, in authority over her.

"We've been married ten years and she continually runs over me. I don't think Crystal has any respect for men. I can understand her reactions. She's determined that I won't be like her father and treat her the way her mother was treated. But, Pat, I'm not her father. I'm Richard, and I don't want to walk all over her. I want to love her.

"Okay, so I have a lot to learn in the area of romance, but she has some things to learn about respecting me as her husband. I come on like a big macho-type man but it's all show. Crystal has always known that. She twists and turns me like a paper clip. Then she puts me down and refuses to let me move.

"I've searched and tried to do everything the way she wants it done, but she changes her mind and then blames me for not doing it her way. When I try to check things out with her, she gets angry. I would never make a decision on my own. She would break into a rage.

"I've almost lost all my respect as a man except at work. There I get the respect Crystal doesn't give me at home. I need to be treated like a human being."

I glanced at my watch and realized that more than an hour had passed. I didn't need a clanging alarm blasting in my ear to know that Richard had opened a significant area of need in his life. I was in a quandry. Excusing myself, I went to the car and called home. I found that Jill and Jim hadn't finished the school project. In fact, Jill told me it could take several more hours. This particular project was an area beyond my expertise, and Jill was happy to help. She didn't mind if we stayed an extra hour or so.

I reached into the backseat and got out a book I'd been reading and some reference notes and took them with me. Slipping back into the booth, I pulled out my Bible. "Richard, unless you are respected as a human being, you cannot be loved. In James Dobson's excellent book *Love Must Be Tough* he talks about the situation that you are living through."

"I've confessed and repented but it doesn't seem to do any

good. Crystal can always find a glaring area of need within me,''
Richard said.

"Clearly, there is a point that we all must come to where we
examine our own motives and aspirations. But once that exam-
ination is done in openness and honesty before the cleansing
blood of Jesus, we are clean. Before God and man, we are at the
point of receiving respect.

"An old Welsh pastor tells about going into a widow's home
at the turn of the century. She was an invalid, crippled in her feet.
She spent all of her day lying on a mat next to the stove in the
kitchen. Her routine had been repeated for many years. The
crippling disease was spreading throughout her body and pain
was etched across her face.

"The pastor asked if she would like prayer. 'Oh, Pastor,' she
said, 'I need forgiveness, poor, rotten sinner that I am. I can't
have prayer until I have all my sins and unworthiness taken
away.'

"The pastor reached over in compassion and took her tiny
hand. 'Have you come to the saving knowledge of Jesus as your
personal Savior?'

" 'Oh, yes, but I need my sins forgiven.'

" 'Well, when was the last time you asked for forgiveness?'
the preacher quizzed her, believing that they would unearth some
crime which she had committed and had never repented of.

" 'Why, this morning. During my morning devotions, I asked
for forgiveness.'

" 'My, dear,' the preacher asked, 'what terrible thing could
you have done while lying on this mat in those few short hours?'

" 'Nothing. I've committed no crime.'

" 'Then what sin have you been involved in during the morning?'

" 'No sin.'

" 'Then you don't need forgiveness. You're already clean.'

"Richard, while women are particularly prone to being intro-
spective, men can have the same problem. We must come to the
place where we recognize that if we have been cleansed of our
sins, we stand pure and whole before the throne of Mighty God—

not as paupers and beggars but as joint-heirs with Jesus Christ.

" 'It is often the mate who has taken the most offense who suffers from guilt for years should a marriage finally disintegrate','' Dobson asserts.

" 'Questions plague him or her continually. *What did I do wrong? How could I have changed? Where did I fail?* It doesn't matter that the mate was the one who went to the marriage counselor, read all the books, searched, prayed and pleaded. *Surely, there was something I could've done. What was it?'* "

I thought of an incident which involved a friend of mine, William. At age sixty-five, William was a man too young in spirit to retire. Of course, William didn't know how awful it would be for him until he had given up his job as personnel manager of his company and spent three miserable months at home.

When a position working in a small, growing office opened, he grabbed it. He is administrative assistant to the president and does everything from answering the phone to hiring new personnel. One afternoon, after almost a year of working, he called me on the phone. When the opening politeness was over, William became serious. "I'm going to quit my job," he said with a plaintive tone in his voice.

"What's wrong? I thought you believed that God gave you this position."

I remembered the day that William had explained to me how God had opened the door. I couldn't understand this turn of events. "What's happened? Is it the job? Your boss?"

"No. Not my job, and my boss, Frank, is a good, godly man. I respect him in business, but to be honest, it's his wife.

"She is helpless. She calls her husband at least five times a day. There is no decision that she can make on her own. I haven't been nosy or prying, but she will usually talk with me before I get him on the line. The last few weeks Frank has been out of town for the company, and she has become more and more dependent on me.

"Now, I'm not talking about important decisions. I mean, what will the children wear to school? Is it all right for her to go out to lunch with a friend? At first, it was humorous. Now, it's not funny. I'm concerned that when her husband returns, she'll continue to consult me about these trivial matters. I'm old enough to be her father, but I'm not her father, and I don't like making childish decisions for an adult who is approaching thirty years old.''

"Richard, we often set ourselves up for failure just like this poor woman who can make no decisions did. In the book *When Smart People Fail,* authors Carole Hyatt and Linda Gottlieb cite an absence of commitment as one of the leading reasons for failure in a life. Often we cushion ourself against failure by never really trying to succeed.

"You say you need to be treated like a man. Then act like one. Like this young wife and mother who had come to depend on William, we can leave every decision up to someone else and never answer the questions ourselves. If we don't ever put ourselves on the line, we can always say that we didn't really care anyway.

" 'The imaginary terrors of failure loom so large that noncommitters try to prevent failure by not involving themselves emotionally. Of course, what they're doing by their halfhearted actions is increasing the likelihood of their downfall,' said Hyatt and Gottlieb.

"They concluded, 'People who lack self-esteem, although they may say all the right things, often say them with a question mark in their voice.'

"Even though Jill suffered from a low self-image, she always demanded that I respect her as a person. She could and did make decisions for herself and the family. I knew that this was a godly seed and I never tried to hamper that growth. In fact, I tried to encourage Jill in every way possible.

"Titus 2:15 says not to let anyone 'despise' you. One commentary says that in today's terminology, we would have to translate this sentence, 'Don't let people push you around.'

"A study of the Greek shows that the word translated 'despised' means 'contempt felt in the mind which is displayed in injurious action.' Paul used the same word when he wrote to Timothy and said, 'Do not let any despise your youth but be an example in word, in conversation, in faith, in spirit and in purity.' (*See* 1 Timothy 4:12.)

"In chapter two, Paul instructed Titus, '. . . say "No" to ungodliness and worldly passions, and to live self-controlled, upright and godly lives in this present age, while we wait for the blessed hope—the glorious appearing of our great God and Savior, Jesus Christ, who gave himself for us to redeem us from all wickedness and to purify for himself a people that are his very own, eager to do what is good' (Titus 2:12–14 NIV).

"Paul continues on to say that we must not allow others to despise us. In speaking against wickedness and being eager to do what is good, Paul concludes the passage by his injuncture not to submit to those forces which are exhibited in others and try to destroy us.

"Richard, there are guidelines in dealing with Crystal which you need to understand. First, you are not wrestling with flesh and blood but with spiritual forces and principalities. Crystal is not your problem. No one else is driving you to distraction. Your battle is a spiritual one and can only be won by the rules of godliness and truth.

"Second, there is no place for humanistic assertiveness in your life. Our position in the heavenly kingdom has been given to us by God and there is no place for pride. We did not earn or deserve the free gift of grace that Jesus gave to us. Therefore, humility must accompany every action.''

"Third, there are positive actions which you can take. They are found in Titus 2:7, 8 (NIV): 'In everything set them an example by doing what is good. In your teaching show integrity, seriousness and soundness of speech that cannot be condemned.'

"The positive actions we draw from these verses are: *Do what is good*. Some things may not appear important until you realize that they are molding the well-being of our families.''

"That's true," Richard inserted, "I've overheard my mother confess that during the first twenty years that my parents were married, she anticipated my dad's every desire. She fixed his dinner plate, picked up his underwear, made and poured his coffee, got up and prepared snacks while he was relaxing, and tended to the children. There was no task too small for her to perform.

"Mom did it because she loved my dad and wanted to please him. After all, she reasoned, she didn't have a job outside the home, and she knew that when he came home he was tired and needed some space.

"Once the children were grown, it dawned on both Mom and Dad that he had become an invalid in their home. I don't mean that he couldn't walk, but he was as crippled in the kitchen as if he were confined to a wheelchair. Dad had no idea where anything was kept. He couldn't even make a peanut butter and jelly sandwich if he were faced with a starving gunman demanding food.

"If anything had happened to my mother, Dad would've been totally lost. One afternoon Dad confessed that he didn't believe that he could survive without Mother and he was terrified.

"Mom had thought she was doing him good by anticipating his every need. Over the years, she had made him so dependent on her that the result was fearful. From that day on, Dad began to be more self-sufficient."

"That's exactly what I mean," I said, "but humans are an odd mixture, aren't we?"

"While I was guarding myself against becoming a man like Crystal's father, I allowed Satan to rob me of my self-respect," Richard said.

"That leads us to the next thing you must do: *Show integrity and be consistent in the way you live,*" I said, going back to the ways that Richard could regain his lost self-esteem. "Then: *Realize that your life is a serious business.* You are having far-reaching influence on your family and friends; and *Make sure that the words you speak are sound in common sense and kindness.*

"Dr. Dobson explains that, 'successful marriages usually rest on a foundation of accountability between husbands and wives. They reinforce responsible behavior in one another by a divinely inspired system of checks and balances. In its absence, one party may gravitate toward abuse, insult, accusation, and ridicule of the other, while his or her victim placidly wipes away the tears and mutters with a smile, "Thanks, I needed that!"

Richard sat for a minute then got up to pay the check. "I've got a lot to chew on. I know that I need two things from Crystal: I need her respect and I need her love. Tonight, I've realized that I also need a third thing. I need to begin to seek God in a new way. There are answers in the Bible that I didn't know were there."

Richard playfully slapped me on the back as we left. "Thanks, I needed that," he said with a broad grin.

Chapter Eight

Hidden Behind This Face Is Me

In the mornings after I've taken the children to school and Pat has gone for his daily jog, we have an hour or more before he has to go to the office. Sometimes, I prepare a large breakfast and we take an extra few minutes with our second glass of juice. More often, we have an informal breakfast of cereal, milk, and toast, which gives us more time to be together.

On the morning after Pat's talk with Richard in the coffee shop, I took the children to school and came back in a twit. Without examining my reactions, I came into the house, slammed down my carryall, and headed for the kitchen.

Pat came out from the back of the house. He had showered and was ready for a morning of pleasant conversation. I was in no mood for common courtesies, however. I stalked and slammed while preparing a breakfast of poached eggs and cracked wheat and bran muffins. Trying to penetrate through my wall of irritation, Pat talked about the things he and Richard had discussed the night before. I listened halfheartedly, but inside there was unconscious anger. It was like an itch that I couldn't find to scratch.

Finally, Pat realized that there was no redeeming the morning. He had tried almost everything up his masculine sleeve to relieve the mounting tension. Before he left for the office, he called me to the door and gave me a kiss. "Do you want to tell me what's wrong?" he said in a firm voice which showed no threat of anger.

I had honestly not realized that anything was wrong. I knew I was irritated. I knew that nothing seemed to be going right, but I had not consciously seen that I was hurting. I stared at Pat for a few seconds and then started to bite my lip, trying to hold back the tears. "Not one of my children kissed me good-bye this morning," I said.

"But things were hectic."

"I've been trying to take that into account, but not one of them kissed me." By now the tears were trickling down my cheeks. Pat reached over and wiped them away using both thumbs.

I recounted that Jim and Bob had carried Jim's science project into his classroom at the junior high school. I offered to help them take the larger piece of aquarium, but they insisted they didn't need me.

Then when we arrived at the elementary school, Andrea and Sarah saw a friend who had been absent for several days. They leaped out of the van almost before I had applied the brakes.

Thomas was lecturing Stephen on the fine art of folding and flying a paper airplane. They were in their own world of arts and science which hardly left room to notice their mother sitting behind the steering wheel.

Bob and Karyn had misplaced one of Bob's homework papers and were frantically sorting through their notebooks and texts. I never could figure how Karyn had become involved in the search. When they finally found the mischievous roving math paper, Bob held it up and cheered while Karyn scolded him about being more careful. They were almost late by this time and bolted out the front door of the van without even a backward glance.

Putting his briefcase down, Pat took me in his arms and held me until I had cried the hurt out of my system. In a few minutes, I was fine and able to face the world again. "Thank you," I said as he released me.

He drove out the driveway while I went into the kitchen with an improved outlook. By the time the dishwasher was loaded with the breakfast plates, the phone rang. Wiping the soap suds from my hands, I was surprised at the pleasant tone in my voice when I answered the phone. Crystal was on the other end and wondered if she could stop by the house at ten o'clock to show me something special.

I kept busy with the details of straightening up the house while Michael played with his toy train in the family room. When Crystal breezed in, I was out in the utility room with my head stuck in the freezer, planning our evening meal. Because I didn't hear her knocking on the door, I was surprised by her sudden appearance in that part of the house. Michael had recognized her from the front window and had answered the door. Crystal was grinning as she held a baby girl that I guessed to be about thirteen months old.

"This is Kara; I'm going to take care of her while her mom is working," Crystal said, turning Kara around so that I could see her face.

She had been crying and her bottom lip stuck out like a park bench, but Kara was a beautiful, healthy child. The blond hair and brown eyes produced a contrast that made her most appealing. While her facial features weren't especially attractive by worldly standards, there was a beauty that shone through her personality.

I reached out to take her, and to my surprise Kara responded to me immediately with a smile. As I took her into my arms, Crystal said, "Jill, I'm so happy. I can't believe how cooperative Richard has been about my taking care of Kara. Of course, I guess if I were honest, I would have to admit that I eventually get what I want, but this time it was really easy. Usually it takes weeks of

planning and preparation to soften Richard. All I had to do this
time was ask, and he was willing to allow me to keep a child. It's
hard to believe.''

''Perhaps the Lord is trying to teach both of us something
about being open and honest,'' I said. Kara's park-bench bottom
lip had reminded me of my own performance with Pat this
morning.

''What do you mean? You and Pat have your marriage all
together.''

''Basically, yes, but Crystal, we do blow it, you know. This
morning I was acting like an irritable, old warhorse until Pat
called me short and made me tell him what was wrong. The
interesting part was that I'd not stopped to examine why I was
feeling hurt until Pat forced me. Yet once I was able to open up
and share, I felt like facing the world again.''

At that point in the conversation, four-year-old Michael came
up to touch and caress baby Kara. I sat down in the chair so that
Michael could reach her. ''Be tender,'' I said as a reminder.
Michael cooed and petted the baby.

''Have you ever noticed a small boy with a tiny child? Almost
without exception, boys will show an enormous amount of gentleness and affection, even more so than little girls,'' Crystal
mused. ''I wonder what happens in a young man's life to change
all that.''

''What do you mean?''

''How many men do you know who would show their wives
that kind of affection?'' Crystal asked, motioning to Michael.
''Richard seems able to show me tenderness only during our
times together when we're having sexual intercourse.''

''Have you tried to be open with Richard about how you
feel?'' I asked while we continued to watch Michael and Kara.
He had started to caress her cheeks and kiss her hands.

''Not any more. When we were dating, we were able to talk.
I remember one night my best friend and I had an argument. She
had slammed down the phone only minutes before he came to
pick me up for our date. I was miserable and he insisted that I tell
him what was wrong. By the time I finished telling him about the

conversation, he took my hand and kissed it just the way Michael is doing with Kara. I think that was the moment I fell in love with him.

"Now, he doesn't even want to talk to me—except to talk about his work. I get weary of hearing about steel tie-beams and office procedures."

My ears perked up because Crystal had ventured into an area vital to their relationship. "Do you understand how important Richard's career is to him?"

"I suspect it's more important than the children and me," Crystal said with sarcasm.

"Do you think you could ever come to look on Richard's career as a part of your life together, instead of competition?"

A puzzled expression spread across Crystal's face. "I don't grasp where you're headed," she admitted.

"Remember we talked weeks ago about the fact that there are some things that we cannot change. Richard will always love his job. You need to accept that as a fact. Crystal, I've fought this battle within myself. Believe me, give it up now before you become weary with it.

"A man derives a great deal of his self-approval from his vocation. Much of his self-worth and ego hinges on how well he is able to function at work. God said in the Scriptures that if a man does not provide for his family, he has denied the faith and is worse than an infidel. Those are strong words. There is a part of Richard that will always need the acceptance he is afforded in the confines of the workplace.

"The Reverend Lane Adams says that a man's approach to life tends to be vocation-centered and headfirst. On the other hand, Dr. Heather Remoff researched to find what male characteristics were attractive to women. Her findings revealed that a woman is attracted to a man who is a good provider and aggressive and who has good income potential and control over material resources. Those things were important to me when I was looking for a mate. Were they to you?"

"Of course," Crystal said, surprised that I would question such obvious points.

"Then why fight Richard's career with such vigor now that you're married? The characteristics you consider so distasteful in him now are the very things which attracted you. For you and Richard to be truly happy with each other, you must be fulfilled within yourselves. A sense of accomplishment in doing a job well will build that needed positive self-image.

"It's important that you help Richard keep a proper perspective and balance, but there's a balance for you also. Richard's job is important for him and for your family. Choose to become a part of that area of his life. When he wants to discuss work, listen."

"I understand your point, Jill, but it's more than that. He doesn't want to listen to me. When I try to tell him about a special event, he always responds with the same line, 'Get to the point!'

"Sometimes, I don't have a point. Often, I merely want to tell him about an experience. I want him to share a good thing with me or maybe even a miserable experience. But he has to have a solution to every situation. I don't want a solution. There are times when he tells me how to settle a problem before he even knows what I'm talking about. I want him to listen, take my hand, and kiss my fingers." Crystal's eyes were riveted on Michael.

"I don't understand what I'm hearing. You want Richard to open up. But because he isn't open to you, you've decided to close yourself to him. Does that make sense?"

Michael had wandered back into the family room to play with his train, and Crystal reached over to take Kara from me. "It makes sense not to risk being hurt," she said as she picked up the diaper bag to leave.

"All he wants from me is sex anyway. I think it would shock him to know that my sexual response or what I agree to do sexually with him has almost no bearing on how I feel about him as a person.

"Anyway, Jill, I don't think that you know me as well as you think. I can be horrible to Richard when I become frustrated. The only time he pays attention to me is when I get angry. So I get angry to get his attention. I'll pick up a plate or something and throw it. It always works, too. But I don't want to be like that. I hate myself when I've treated him badly.

"Jill, I want to tell Richard that hidden behind this face is me. I'm a person. A woman lives in this body, and he would benefit a lot by getting to know me."

"Why don't you tell him that?" I asked.

"I couldn't," Crystal said, feigning firmness, but I saw a whimsical smile creep over her face.

"Why not? Hit him with the element of surprise."

By now, her mind was churning with the possibilities. I could tell because a smile had spread over her face, and there was a delightful twinkle in her eyes. "I wonder what would happen if I looked him in the eyes and told him that he didn't know what a good deal he was missing by not getting to know me better."

"Crystal, you might have to be patient. It won't happen overnight, but I think that you and Richard are ready to open up and begin to listen to each other. Remember, being open and developing a relationship could be a whole new thing for Richard."

"It is a new thing. He hasn't had a good friend since he was in high school, and he's even lost contact with his old football buddies. When all his friends went to college or got jobs, they didn't even bother to write to each other or visit. There isn't anyone at work that he talks to."

I encouraged her, "Give it time. If Richard is like most men, he hasn't shared any emotional feelings since before he was an adolescent. It's going to take patience from you."

Crystal put the diaper bag down and repositioned the baby on one hip. "Can you give me some tips on how to be open with him?"

"Well, Richard has given you a clue. He wants to hear the 'bottom line' first. I think every man says that to his wife. When Pat would tell me to get to the punch line, I thought he wasn't interested in hearing the details of my story. But that isn't true. He wants to hear it in reverse order from the way I tell most stories. I love a novel to build up to a climax. That's how I would tell Pat a story. He wanted to hear the juicy part in the beginning. Then he was ready for me to fill him in on all the nitty gritty.''

"Like a newspaper story?" Crystal asked.

"What do you mean?" I quizzed her.

"Remember in school," Crystal reminded me, "we learned how to write a newspaper article? You give the most important facts first. Who, what, where, and when. Then you proceed to fill in the details in descending order of importance.''

"That's right—like a pyramid," I said, recalling my college journalism class.

I continued, "Another thing I've found to be useful for me is to remember that I'm assisting Pat by helping him to acquire a useful skill when I talk with him and share my feelings. Listening is a skill that few men value.

"It's like when my mother taught me how to knit," I said. "As a child, I couldn't understand why she took such a long time to teach me how to hold the thread. It wasn't until I'd become quite proficient that I appreciated her insistence that I acquire that basic skill before I went on to learn the stitches.

"Competition is the overriding factor in many men's lives. As his wife, you can become his helpmate by assisting him in learning to listen. The reason he wants to give you solutions is because he thinks that you feel the same pressure to win. He's trying to assist you in accomplishing your goal. As you help him to learn listening skills, he will have one of the most valuable tools within himself that he will ever possess.

"The third thing to watch for is the nonverbal communications which speak to us all the time. For example, each evening as we prepare for our evening meal, I light the two large candles which are positioned in the middle of our large, Williamsburg dining table. Usually Sarah, our eight-year-old, will position herself by the light switch. Once the family has taken their places, Sarah will flick off the overhead light. Within a matter of seconds, a miracle of quiet comes over the children.

"With ten people sitting at the same table, you look for any way to keep the fray down. We happened upon our candle-quieter quite by accident. One night, the children and Pat planned a candlelit dinner for me. We all noticed that in the subdued light, everyone was calmer and more peaceful. Even though the conversation ebbed and flowed around the table in the usual manner, everyone spoke in hushed tones to match the gentle flicker of the candles.

"Neither Pat nor I have told the children that they should be more quiet during the evening meal. The candlelight speaks a nonverbal message that is far more eloquent than any speech we could have communicated."

Crystal shifted Kara on her hip, picked up her diaper bag again, and said, "Okay. You've given me three things to help me in opening up to Richard.

"Present the facts first. Then fill in the juicy details.

"Second, I need to remind myself often that I'm being a helper to Richard by assisting him to learn listening skills so that I won't become discouraged if he doesn't want to listen and share with me at the beginning."

I pulled *Homemade,* a small newsletter we receive, from a stack of papers on the table next to the chair where Pat usually sits. Earlier that morning he had shown me an article taken from *As for Me and My House* by Walter Wangerin, Jr. (Thomas Nelson, 1987).

Marriage is not romanticized in the creation account. Its ideal purpose is not one of sweet feelings, tender moods, poetical affections, or physical satisfactions—not "love" as the world defines love in all its nasal songs and its popular shallow stories. . . . Marriage is meant to be flatly practical. One human alone is help*less,* unable. But "two are better than one," says Ecclesiastes, "because they have a good reward for their toil. For if they fall, one will lift the other. . . ." Marriage makes the job of survival possible. . . .

And the fact that a spouse is termed a "helper" declares marriage was never an end in itself but a preparation.

We've accomplished no great thing, yet, in getting married. We have not *completed* a relationship (though many a fool assumes that the hard work's done with the wedding and turns attention to other interests). Rather, we've established the terms by which we now will go to work.

"We all know that God made us to be helpers for our husbands, but I never felt it was a very important position until this minute," Crystal confessed.

I continued, "Third, we need to watch for nonverbal communication clues from our spouse."

"Crystal, you not only want to be able to share your feelings with Richard but you want him to be able to share with you. But feelings are not to be judged. Richard doesn't have to feel the same way you do. He will never cry over the same things you cry over.

"At times, a woman will become superior about her ability to share openly and honestly, or she will become analytical. Most men will recoil from that kind of response.

"Remember, challenges and reproaches will not work with Richard. However, a carefully worded invitation can elicit a response. Richard will answer questions that elicit factual information. Ask Richard about his day and his work. Did he finish the project he is currently working on? Who are the men on his crew? Are they good workers?

"It will be easier for Richard to tell you what he does at work than how he feels about it. Start by asking for facts as an introduction to his feelings. If Richard sees your requests as a participation in his life, he won't look on your questions as an intrusion. He needs to see that you want to know his feelings, not so you can use them against him, but because you want to become more intimately involved with him.

"Be sure that your desire is not to control him but to share with him. When Richard understands the extent of your caring and that you will not use the information he shares as a weapon against him, then he will become more and more open with you."

With one last, tender finger kiss from Michael, Crystal and Kara headed for the door. "Thank you, Michael," Crystal said, tousling his hair, "for reminding me of a part of Richard I had almost forgotten." As Crystal and Kara left, I took Michael in my arms and silently prayed that God would help him to preserve that exquisite tenderness that kisses the fingers of little girls.

Chapter Nine

Open Up

Pat came home early one afternoon to prepare for a business trip. God has gifted Pat with the ability to communicate to large and small groups. The Lord has opened many doors for him to speak before congregations and civic organizations. That afternoon he was to fly out of Orlando to Oregon and come back the next day. I had packed his bags while he rehearsed his message. When he got into the car to leave for the airport, however, the engine of his automobile wouldn't start. The weather had turned blustery cold and rainy. Moisture had probably condensed in the gas tank.

Jill offered to drive me to the airport. I realized, however, that Jill's time was tightly scheduled with activities for the children. Hating to disappoint them, I decided to call Richard and see if he could take me to the airport. I realized that Richard wouldn't be working because of the rain and cold. In addition, I reasoned that this would be a good opportunity to follow up on our previous conversations.

Richard was home and asked if Crystal could ride with us. The airport is about forty-five minutes from our home. They had made plans to go out to dinner at a restaurant across town. Richard agreed to deposit me at the airport, and then they could eat. I welcomed having Crystal with us because I knew that her openness and eagerness to share would facilitate our conversation.

When you begin to communicate feelings with others, there are a myriad of pitfalls you can fall into. Communication is like soap. It comes in many different sizes, shapes, forms, packages, and prices. Not all soap, such as the harsh detergent used in our dishwasher, is good for your skin. Formulas vary in degrees of strength. But soap, every type and brand, has one basic purpose—to keep things clean.

In like manner, there are various forms of communication, but all have one common purpose. God gave us communication so that we could maintain contact with other humans. That contact can take a multitude of expressions—from the simple smile of passing strangers to the intimate whisper of lovers.

For centuries, the use of words has been considered the epitome of communication. In recent years, we have realized that words only scratch the surface in personal communication. The tone of voice and our body language also tell volumes about what is going on.

Several years ago, I read an article about body language and was fascinated with the discovery that the way we hold our bodies tells significantly more about what we are saying than the words we speak. I took these profound results home to Jill. "So . . ." she said, without lifting an eye from her needlepoint project. "I've known that for years. Every woman knows about body language. What's the big secret? I can't believe anyone would even bother to write about it."

Most women are like Jill and have instinctively realized that *the way* they speak is more important to their family than the words they say.

Recently I read in H. Norman Wright's *Understanding the Man in Your Life* that science has shown that men and women differ in the way they use their brains. In some ways women have an advantage over men. A woman's brain is not specialized, whereas a man's brain is. The whole brain of a woman operates at the same time. A man must shift from one side of his brain to the other. This ability to compartmentalize allows a man to focus all of his attention on the one project he is absorbed in.

His wife uses both sides of her brain simultaneously to work on a problem. The left and right side operate in harmony and cooperation. Some of the left-brain abilities are duplicated in her right brain and some of the right brain in the left. Women also have large connectors between the two sides when they are born and thus can integrate information more skillfully.

God made a woman this way because He knew that she would need to attend to a ten-year-old repairing his bicycle with a butcher knife in the garage, a toddler learning how to do dishes on a stool at the kitchen sink, a baby nursing, her pedigreed miniature poodle trying to mate with a Doberman pinscher in the backyard, the telephone ringing, and a broccoli-cheese soufflé burning in the oven—all at the same time.

In the meantime, her husband can be absolutely oblivious to the noise and clamor because he is reading the paper or watching sports on TV.

As a natural consequence, women are more perceptive about people than men. They have a greater ability to pick up feelings and sense the differences in what people say, discerning more accurately what they actually mean.

God understands that while words are important, they are not the only form, nor the most complete form, of real communication. As an illustration, think back to when Adam and Eve sinned. God came to the garden and found no one. He called to Adam, who was hiding behind a bush. Adam didn't say that he had sinned, but God knew. How did He know?

We rationalize to ourselves, "Of course, God knew Adam had sinned. He is God." Yet, let's suppose for a few seconds that God—for Adam's sake, in order to communicate with him—had divested Himself of a minute portion of His godliness in order to reach down to Adam's level to be his friend. And suppose, only for the sake of understanding a microscopic portion of God's mighty heart, that on the day Adam sinned, a TV camera was able to record some of God's feelings . . .

All day God has looked forward to a refreshing stroll with His two friends. This quiet time has become the highlight of His eternal existence. One afternoon, He comes down from heaven and, instantly, He is on the familiar path that He and Adam have walked together since Adam's creation.

Recently, since Adam's wife, Eve, had been formed, the three of them have shared even more intimacy. Because Adam's loneliness has ceased, there is a total contentment in everything he and Eve do together, which pleases God.

God stoops down and touches a yellow flower growing next to a stone while he waits in anticipation for His friends to appear. In a few moments, He realizes that something is wrong—fearfully wrong. Adam has always waited for Him on the pathway. Each day, after their walk, Adam and Eve watched Him ascend into heaven; and there they would be the next evening, waiting for Him where they had last parted.

Suddenly, God senses a presence. Someone is watching. He turns, but no one is there. "Adam," He calls, "where are you?"

Silence.

Like a mother who realizes that she hasn't heard from her child in several minutes, God knows that there has been trouble in the Garden. "Adam, where are you?" From behind a tree two pairs of fearful eyes peer out at Him. No words need to be spoken; God knows. His enormous heart is pierced with the knowledge that their fellowship has been shattered.

In his silence, Adam has spoken volumes. Adam has revealed his sin. With a deep, abiding sorrow beyond the understanding of mortal man, God asks, "Adam, what have you done?"

As we study and meditate on the Genesis account of man's fall, we come to comprehend that our scenario could well be more fact than fiction. Adam screamed his sinfulness to God with his silence.

As I loaded my overnight bag into Richard's trunk and got into the backseat of their car, Crystal looked at me with a rather wary eye. Her body language was speaking to me. This was a woman who was not happy with the turn of events; however, I didn't know what the problem was. Immediately, I felt that this trip to the airport had been an intrusion on their dinner plans.

I wondered if Richard had consulted with her about taking me to the airport across town or if he had assumed that she wouldn't care. As often is the case, I could identify with Richard's feelings. He had no idea how important a dinner with her husband can be to a wife. To him, taking me to the airport was an act of kindness toward a friend. To Crystal, it was an act of betrayal and an insult.

During the first ten years of our marriage, one of Jill's favorite prods for me was to cut off verbal communication for hours or days. Often her silence had been preceded by an unspoken insult from me. One of the things that hurt her more than anything else was to be emotionally dismissed from my mind. She would be sharing the details of a wedding she had attended when, in the middle of one of her sentences, I would unconsciously reach over and turn on the television or turn up the volume of the radio.

Without my saying a word, Jill knew that she had been left standing beside the bridesmaid in her pink organdy dress with its lovely brushed satin sash and I had become an active participant in World News Tonight.

As I buckled my seat belt, I couldn't help but remember the times Jill and I had scheduled a trip and looked forward to it, only to have the events of the afternoon shattered by a thoughtless act.

Jill always looked forward to going to speaking engagements with me because the drive there and back meant that we would have an hour or two to be together. Before we had gotten out of the driveway, she would seize on the quietness of the moment to talk. As with most women, details are important to Jill, and we would be deep into a blow-by-blow description, when I would suddenly realize it was time for the results of a football game. I'd nonchalantly reach over and turn on the radio as though I were the only person traveling in the car. That action said to Jill that she was not important to me. Her thoughts and ideas were not worth wasting my time.

As I have begun to look for ways to communicate with Jill, she and I have come upon some interesting observations. Most non-verbal communication is not a conscious act. It comes from the subconscious area of our lives. During those years when I was constantly turning Jill off by turning on the radio, I did not understand why she became angry.

In truth, I was not consciously aware of the attitude behind my actions. I would readily admit that I wasn't interested in her details, but I never wanted to hurt Jill. Because the things she was describing were of no consequence to me, I assumed they were also not important to her and, therefore, Jill would not get her feelings hurt if I didn't listen.

Unwilling to allow our trip to the airport to become unpleasant because of a misunderstanding, I decided to meet the challenge head-on. "I guess you weren't very happy about having to take me to the airport," I ventured to Crystal.

"I'm not angry with you," Crystal snapped, glaring at Richard with a look that could've scorched the brain of a codfish.

"True, but you aren't happy about taking me to the airport," I said, trying to be as nonchalant as possible.

"What difference does it make? Richard wouldn't talk to me anyway. Why should I even be concerned? He doesn't care about me or the things I say."

"Crystal, that's enough," Richard said firmly but defensively.

"Wait a minute, Richard. Maybe this time, Crystal needs to talk. Isn't the next step to open up?"

"Crystal opens up . . ." Richard began.

". . . and you clam up!" Crystal finished his sentence with a loud interruption.

"Hey, I'm not a very good referee for a fight, but maybe I could help you. It sounds as though you are experiencing some of the same problems with communicating that Jill and I have had.

"Richard, you will listen to Crystal to a certain point, but then you cut her off."

"Well, that's what she says. I don't go around trying to hurt her, but I don't see why I should be interested in every tweet uttered by the sparrow who's nesting outside our bedroom window.''

"Therefore, in the middle of my sentence, you turn on the TV or sit like a lump of dough waiting to rise.''

"Does it help to know that you aren't the only couple who has struggled with this situation? Lane Adams says we all get married expecting that our mates will tend to respond to any given set of circumstances in the same way we do. When they don't, it comes as quite a shock and surprise.''

I quoted to them from an article I was reading. Reverend Adams asserts, "Given a succession of these 'strange' reactions to a series of situations, you have each party beginning to be persuaded that he or she married a very strange person. No, each just married a member of the opposite sex.

". . . Nobody has warned any of us of just how different men and women really are. When we run into that difference in actual fact, we falsely assume that only our particular mate is afflicted with this sort of weird response to what seems to be a very simple situation.''

"Richard,'' I said, "it's easy to fall into the habit of not appearing to listen. Yet, Crystal, it seems that you are more responsive to Richard's body language than to what he says.

"A few weeks ago, I came home from work. On the way from the office, I had gone by the children's school as usual and picked up three of the boys from basketball practice.

"While heading out the door of the school, I ran into one of the trustees. I asked him a question concerning the next year at the school. His answer had been exciting to me as a parent. I came into the house anxious to share with Jill.

"Unfortunately, by the time I arrived home, Jill was involved in the last-minute details of dinner preparations. As I talked with Jill, she continued to walk back and forth from the stove to the dining room, putting the hot dishes of food on the table. Undaunted, I followed Jill, turning as she turned, helping where I could, and chattering away. Suddenly, Jill stopped and asked, 'This is really important to you, isn't it?'

" 'Yes, it is, Jill. I want you to hear about this,' I said with the earnestness of a man who had come to deliver a prophetic word.

"I didn't have to tell Jill that my conversation with the trustee was important; my actions gave Jill a signal which spoke louder than words. Jill stopped in the middle of the kitchen with a steaming pan of chicken held between two hot pads, 'I want to hear this, Pat,' she said, 'but supper will be cold if I don't get it on the table. Do you mind if I continue to work?'

"Well, I was beginning to wonder if she was interested, but when she acknowledged me and asked the question, I didn't care if she was working. She put the food on the table and I continued to follow her, recounting the details of our conversation."

"You mean you didn't get your feelings hurt because Jill wasn't listening to you?" Crystal asked, half in sarcasm and half interested.

"No," I answered honestly. "I normally don't become intimidated or turned off when Jill doesn't put her whole heart and soul into what I'm saying. You can listen and walk, too. While I've tried to become more aware of the signals Jill could be giving by her actions, I don't jump to a negative conclusion before giving her a chance to explain.

"Another important thing Jill and I have learned is that we don't assume that we know what the other person is thinking or planning. A harsh tone of voice may not mean that I'm angry. It probably is a signal that I've had a stressful day.

"Gloria B. Casey once wrote, 'Love talked about can be easily turned aside, but love demonstrated is irresistible.'

"In the same way that negative communication can be transmitted to each other, love can be demonstrated as well as spoken to our mates.

"First Peter 3:1–5 (NIV) says, 'Wives, in the same way be submissive to your husbands so that, if any of them do not believe the word, they may be won over without words by the behavior of their wives, when they see the purity and reverence of your lives. Your beauty should not come from outward adornment, such as braided hair and the wearing of gold jewelry and fine clothes. Instead, it should be that of your inner self, the unfading beauty of a gentle and quiet spirit, which is of great worth in God's sight. For this is the way the holy women of the past who put their hope in God used to make themselves beautiful.'

"Jill and I gleaned from these verses that there are five things which are irresistible in communication: purity, reverence, gentleness, a quiet spirit, and hope. They are demonstrations of love.

"While none of these virtues depends on verbal skills or the words spoken, they are our most valuable tools in reaching down to draw things from each other which help us to share more effectively."

As Richard skillfully weaved through the traffic, I could see Crystal's glare soften. Even though Richard was concentrating on his driving, he stole a quiet glance at her. As briefly as possible, I explained to them the five important principles Peter talked about.

Purity

The pristine attitude that shouts, "I don't smoke, and I don't chew, and I don't go with the boys that do," is not what Peter had in mind. It's easy to pay lip service to a set of values and morals. True purity, however, comes from a humble heart that understands the true nature of God and the awful depravity of mankind. This heart is aware that only by falling before God can our motives and actions be pure.

Often, a woman will make her husband into an idol. Her heart is bent toward him in a way that God never intended. As Jill and I look back, Jill realizes that she had built a fantasy world in which Pat Williams was the hero and she was the heroine.

Jill admits that though she knew Jesus was her Savior and Lord, her heart had become hard when she felt that her prayers for me were not going to be answered.

The attitude of every believer must become like Peter's. During Jesus' earthly ministry there came a time that many of the crowd who had been following Jesus turned from Him. Jesus questioned the twelve disciples, "Will you leave me, too?"

Peter's answer was profoundly simple: "To whom can we turn? Only you have the words of life."

It isn't important to have all the answers, but it is essential to know the One who has the words of life. True purity comes from a heart that is willing to set aside our own programs and look to Jesus as Lord.

Reverence

Before we were married, Jill was a schoolteacher. From the moment she stepped into a classroom full of students, she was the TEACHER—the general in charge. Every student in the room understood that she would be obeyed and respected. There was an awareness within her that once the children knew she was the boss, peace and calm would reign in the room. Only after the children had firmly established in their minds that she was to be obeyed could she become their friend.

Jill saw many disastrous classes in which the teacher wanted to be a buddy and friend from the beginning. The children always took advantage, and before many weeks, the classroom became a battleground between the children and the teacher, who competed for control.

Reverence means that we have settled for all time who is the Boss. Our General is Jesus. He is to be obeyed and respected. Only after we have submitted to Him as Master and Absolute Authority do we have the right to become His friend.

Within our private devotional life, there must be a continual understanding that Jesus is King of the universe and that it is a privilege to be counted among His friends.

Gentleness

A friend who has observed our family together several times told Jill and me that the thing that impressed her the most about us was the gentleness of our children. Four of them, the twins (Stephen and Thomas), eight-year-old Sarah, and seven-year-old Andrea, are of Korean descent. The Koreans are known to be a gentle people. But our friend was impressed that Jim, Bob, Karyn, and Michael were equally as tender.

When Bob, who is eleven, helps the little girls with their coats, he doesn't yank or demand. Jim, fourteen, opens the doors for Jill even when she doesn't have an armload of school supplies and jackets.

As I looked at our family, I had to admit that gentleness is a special ingredient we share. Perhaps the gentleness seen by the children has been attractive to them because it comes from strength and is seasoned with large doses of humor.

Neither Jill nor I are ashamed of our love. We want everyone to know that God has done something special for us. That knowledge has given us strength in the face of adversity.

At the same time, we've walked through some deep waters and that pain has helped us value the joy we have even more. We hold the priceless treasure of being able to have a joyful spirit carefully—not out of fear—but with great appreciation.

A Quiet Spirit

The enemies of a quiet spirit are found in 1 Peter 2:1 (NIV). "Therefore, rid yourselves of all malice and all deceit, hypocrisy, envy, and slander of every kind."

When our home blossomed from five to ten people in four years, Jill found that an interesting metamorphosis took place within all of us. We didn't have as much *time* for feelings of malice, deceit, hypocrisy, envy, and slander. We were too busy organizing and keeping the household in order. While outside, circumstances became more hectic; inside, quietness grew.

In *Restoring Your Spiritual Passion* (Oliver Nelson, 1986) Gordon MacDonald wrote, "Perhaps we are always children and don't wish to admit it. Sometimes we feel alone; at other times we are weary from our futile attempts to succeed or improve our lot; on yet other occasions our sense is that of complete vulnerability before the critic or the rival. We come to crave the safe place, a refuge where we can restore our strength, gain our bearings, and begin again."

The quiet spirit has found that refuge within the knowledge

that circumstances may change, but God is steadfast and unmoving.

Hope

When hope is lost, life ceases. In studies done among the terminally ill, it was found that those men and women who never lose the hope that they will survive make the best patients. The paradox is that they also die with more peace and serenity.

Saying that someone has false hope is like ordering "cold, hot apple pie" at your favorite restaurant. A pie can be served hot or cold, not both. Hope is never false. Hope is the one ingredient that keeps a man alive and moving.

As long as you are alive, you must understand that hope should not be lost. Mary Slessor was one of the first missionaries to Africa. She stood before tribal kings and spoke powerful words which changed the hearts of whole villages.

Mary's childhood, however, had not been a happy one. Her alcoholic father had robbed the family of their home, food, clothing, and sense of dignity. Mary came to know Jesus as her Savior as a young woman, and that spark gave her hope in the middle of hardship.

Working in a factory at the age of eleven, Mary had a higher goal in mind. She kept hope alive. It's little wonder that her life had such an impact.

As Richard steered the car into the airport parking lot, I realized that I had more than an hour before my flight. I started to get out of the car, wondering if I had spoiled their evening together by asking for a ride to my plane.

Crystal reached toward my hand. "You've got a few minutes. Don't rush out of the car. I want to apologize for my attitude. When Richard said that we were going to take you to the airport, I saw that as another way for him to get out of being alone with me."

"But that wasn't true," Richard interjected, genuinely surprised by Crystal's confession. "I thought you'd like to have a talk with Pat."

Crystal nodded, "I was reading too much into what you did. Richard and Pat, I'm sorry. I'm glad that we had this time. There is so much for me to learn about marriage and commitment."

"During times of discouragement and failure, all of us wonder if we are ever going to be able to communicate with our mates in a way that will be pleasing to God," I reassured her. "We can be encouraged, however, knowing that if we turn our thoughts and actions over to His control, He will provide ways in which we can show our love. Our communication can be pleasing to our mates as we become pleasing to the Lord."

As Richard and Crystal drove away, they were smiling and holding hands. I headed for my plane and Oregon.

Chapter Ten

Okay, I'll Go First

If one day of the week could be bottled like perfume, I think I'd like to have an ounce of "Essence à la Saturday." It is a day of paradoxes—our laziest, yet most hectic, day. It's a family time, but some Saturdays we are pulled in ten different directions at once.

One Saturday, we recently had a friend visiting from out of town. My parents were arriving from the east coast of Florida. Jim had a basketball game in a town about twenty minutes from Orlando. Bob had two basketball games. One was at 9:00 A.M. and the other one at 2:00 P.M. Karyn had a gymnastics meet, and Stephen and Thomas also had a 10:00 A.M. game.

In fact, in the few short months since Stephen and Thomas have become a part of our family, they've both gotten excited about all American sports, even though they had never seen any kind of organized sports in Korea.

Soccer immediately emerged as Stephen's great love. He is the more aggressive of the twins and feels at home on the competitive field. With dark, expressive eyes and thin features, Stephen and Thomas are perky and energetic eight-year-olds. They arrived from Korea in May of 1987, and quickly acclimated themselves to our family.

That Saturday, however, Stephen's true love, soccer, would be shoved to the backseat. He scored all of the points in the basketball game. Pat and Thomas came home, patting Stephen on the back and proclaiming him the best player of the game.

Like most twins, the older twin is the dominant personality. Pat and I have felt from the first day that we met the boys that Stephen is the older twin. We have no documentation, however. Thomas graciously takes a backseat to the leader. It's rare for Thomas to assume a prominent position or to express an opinion different from the one he thinks people want to hear.

Thomas was named for General Thomas Jonathan ("Stonewall") Jackson. Both Pat and I are history enthusiasts. "Stonewall" Jackson is one of our favorite historical figures. Over the years, in referring to and quoting Thomas J. Jackson, I had affectionately dubbed him T. J.

Naturally, I was anxious to adapt my nickname to Thomas. One afternoon, I was driving the children to soccer practice, and they were chattering away in the backseats of the van. The four Korean children were comparing names and talking about their favorite name. Stephen piped up in a strong voice. "I love my name."

T. J. said, rather wistfully, "Mom loves my name."

I couldn't help overhearing the conversation and asked T. J., "Don't you like your name?"

"If I tell you truth, you will cry and cry," T. J. said in his Korean-English. He pulled his index fingers down his cheeks to show my impending tears.

"I won't cry, T. J.," I promised. "What is it about your name that you don't like?"

"Oh, I love Thomas. I don't like T. J. That's not my name. I want you call me Thomas."

Sometimes honesty can be painful to those we love. It took a great step of courage for Thomas to be able to tell me that he didn't like his nickname.

The next morning before the church service, I shared Thomas's confession with Crystal. "I understand his feelings exactly," Crystal admitted. "While I want our marriage to be healed, I don't like the process of being honest with Richard. Sometimes it seems easier to let things ride along in a familiar jaunt instead of being jerked around by the starting and stopping of constructing a new type of relationship.

"I know that the process will be of benefit to Richard and me, but it seems difficult." Before we could continue our conversation, Richard had slipped in between us. The row of seats quickly filled up when our children's Sunday school classes were dismissed and the children filed into church. Pat sat beside me with Jim on his left side.

In the middle of the service, I looked over at Crystal. She was laughing at one of the pastor's illustrations. Richard subconsciously reached over and took her hand. She deliberately squeezed it and smiled at him with a genuine warmth and tenderness.

I sat back, contented that the Lord was repairing their marriage. On the way home from church, I told Pat about my observations. We were both happy about the good things we had seen happening in their marriage.

The events of the morning left me totally unprepared, therefore, for the explosive dynamo who came to our house a few minutes after four o'clock that afternoon.

Crystal had been crying and was clearly more distraught than I had ever seen her. Pat and I had taken a walk around the block and were standing out in the front yard chatting when her small compact car wheeled around the corner. At first it appeared that she wasn't going to stop, but seeing us in the yard, Crystal must have felt obligated or drawn to share the events of the afternoon with us.

We walked over to the car as Crystal got out, slamming the door behind her. She was shaking. From her appearance we couldn't tell if she were distraught from anger or sorrow. When she spoke, however, her fury was blatantly obvious. "I've had it!" she said with her fists clenched. She spoke through her teeth—only her lips moved. "I don't care what you say. This will not work. Richard doesn't want a wife. He wants a machine that can make love and cook his meals.

"He will never be anything other than an obstinate mule of a man." By now, tears were flowing down her cheeks and she was tugging at her nose with a tissue.

Pat took the lead. "Crystal, what's happened? You and Richard seemed all right this morning."

"Seemed is the right word. We *seemed* happy. We always *seem* happy. I feel like a complete fool."

"Come in and have a cup of tea," I said, hoping to calm her down once we were inside. Without another comment, Pat took her by the arm and guided her into the house. While I prepared the drinks, Pat listened.

"This morning after church . . . ," Crystal started, trying to contain her anger once we were seated around the table, because the children were weaving in and out of the dining room to explore the kitchen and family room. Yet her eyes were abrupt reminders of the indignation that burned inside. ". . . after church, I was talking with Mary Beth and William Boggs. William asked me if Richard had gotten the new job he had applied for last week.

"I was stunned because I had no idea that Richard was unhappy with his work. I didn't know that he had applied for another position. I laughed at William and told him that there was no way to know what Richard was doing.

"I laughed, yet I felt betrayed. I hardly know these people and they are better informed about my life than I am. If Richard is planning to change firms, I should be the first one to know—not find out from people who work with him."

I brought the tea to the table. Pat smiled. "Sound familiar?" he asked.

"Crystal, did you know that Pat made two team changes, and I didn't know about either one of them until the contracts were signed? We moved from Chicago to Atlanta and then to Philadelphia. We had to move to another part of the country. In each case, I didn't even know that he was dissatisfied with his present position. There had been drastic upheavals taking place in the teams and in Pat, but I had not been part of any of it—except to move my home and children."

Crystal's eyes widened. "I read that in your book, but I had forgotten."

Pat admitted, "I felt that I wanted to protect Jill from the worry of my misunderstandings with the team owners. I didn't tell her about the drastic changes in my position until I had accepted the new position. It wasn't right, but it was the way I handled crises. I shared almost nothing with her. We both know now that that's a lousy way to live," Pat said.

"And I understand your feelings of betrayal," I assured her.

"I was so angry with Richard that I haven't been able to talk to him at all. I wasn't able to eat my lunch. I prepared the meal and stared at him while he ate. After he and the girls had eaten, Richard began to needle me to tell him what was wrong. My mother came to take the children to the park and I left.

"Hey, he wants me to tell him what's wrong when he is the one who has applied for a position with a new company and hasn't told me. Our whole lives could be changing this very minute and I would have no idea that it was going on if the Boggses had not told me." Crystal's anger had been partially defused by Pat's confession of past misdeeds, but there was still pepper in her expression.

"Can't you talk with him?" I asked, empathizing with her rejection and anger.

"Jill, I don't want to talk to him. If the two of you had not been in the front yard, I would be at my mother's house this minute. I don't plan to take this kind of mental torment the rest of my life. No relationship is worth going through the humiliation that I experienced this afternoon."

"It is worth it if the relationship is a marriage," I said, trying to reassure her.

Pat looked at her with compassion and understanding. "Crystal, sometime during his adolescent years, almost every man in our society begins construction on the castle that becomes his life-style. The building stones consist of anger and a brittle determination not to be hurt by the circumstances of life. Instinct tells a man that becoming a part of the community means that he must suffer with the world. He picks a high hill overlooking his acquaintances as the spot to build his life. The walls of his castle are strong and thick. He digs a moat around it and stocks it with alligators and piranha.

"No one can enter his life except through the drawbridge which lowers and raises at his will. It's a lonely life, to be sure, but a man must protect himself from the feelings and frustrations of hurt at all cost."

Crystal's anger flared again, "What a stupid life. And what about me? How do I get into this castle Richard has built to protect himself from others? From me?"

"That's the problem with castles," Pat continued. "Once the walls have been constructed and the moat dug, it's almost impossible to allow someone else to come into your life. However, Crystal, don't forget the loneliness. No man wants that kind of loneliness."

"And that's where a wife comes into the picture," I inserted. "With encouragement and acceptance, we can help to tear down the walls."

"I don't believe that Richard is lonely. He's too self-sufficient to need anyone."

"That's not what God said about him," Pat interjected.

"What do you mean?"

"The Bible tells us that God looked at Adam and saw no companion suitable for man and, therefore, he made woman for him. It was God's idea that man should not be alone or lonely. Without you, Richard will be lonely."

"Then why does he act as though he doesn't need me?"

"Because Richard has constructed his life-style in the form of a castle, and now he has become its prisoner. God has given you the ability to penetrate those walls and thereby save Richard from his self-imposed loneliness."

"I'm not sure that I can help Richard. I have enough problems of my own without taking on his, too."

"But, Crystal, Pat and I aren't suggesting that you 'take Richard on as a project.' That kind of attitude will never help him.

The worst thing you can do is to make him feel that you have the answers."

". . . or that you have analyzed him and figured out his problems," Pat said. "No. God has made you and Richard into one. Therefore, as you—a singular person standing before God—become healed, Richard will begin to drop the walls of protection and allow God to work in his life also."

"I'm not ready to be the one to start changing," Crystal said with unveiled honesty.

"That is the next step in our plan, ANOINT—**Initiate Change.**"

"Well, that sounded fine four weeks ago," Crystal said, "but now I've seen that there's a huge price to pay in humiliation. I had no idea that my pride would be subjected to such a beating. I'll have to think about it."

Though Pat seldom pressures a person, he took Crystal's hand and said in a firm, though reassuring voice, "Being a part of a family demands that we take our portion of responsibility. As the wife, God has gifted you with some unique gifts. Those gifts can become the catalyst to help Richard see himself and grow into a giving and loving individual.

"Sociologist and historian Carle Zimmerman, in his book *Family and Civilization,* recorded some keen observations about the family as it relates to the disintegration of various cultures. He found some ominous parallels in the family life of all declining cultures. Eight specific patterns emerged in domestic behavior. They are:

1. Marriage loses its sacredness and is broken by divorce.
2. Traditional meaning of the marriage ceremony is lost.
3. Feminist movements abound.
4. Increased public disrespect for parents and authority in general.
5. Acceleration of juvenile delinquency, promiscuity, and rebellion.
6. Refusal of people with traditional marriages to accept family responsibilities.

7. Growing desire for and acceptance of adultery within the society.
8. Increasing interest in and the spread of sexual perversion and sex-related crimes.

"Crystal, many of us find ourselves fitting into that sixth step. We don't want to accept the responsibilities found within the bonds of a marriage. We must begin to accept the conditions inherent within a marriage.

"Right now, God is saying that you are responsible to grow and mature into the best person you can be. No matter who you are married to or in relationship with, you will have the same pressure to maintain maturity within that relationship. In every phase of life, we are faced with a decision to grow as a person. When we take steps toward maturity, then we also grow in our marriage."

"I won't allow Richard to run over me," Crystal said, standing up to leave. The spark of fury was back in her eyes. "I don't care what you say. I won't be a pushover for anyone."

I started to stop Crystal as she stormed out of the house, but Pat put his hand on my arm. "Let her go."

"But, Pat, she doesn't understand what we're saying. Shouldn't we try to explain it to her?"

"This is a large decision for her. The Bible says, 'We die daily.' She won't be able to hear what we are saying until she is able to lay down her will in surrender before the Lord. Unless Crystal is able to give up her preconceived ideas of what God wants for her, she will never be able to grow into a relationship. She'll always be striking out, trying to justify, and finding fault.

"Much of her reaction to Richard stems from the terrible marriage of her parents," I said. "Perhaps when she is fully healed from those early hurts, she'll be able to understand what we're saying."

"Crystal is right, you know," Pat said. "When we come to the place where we say that we are willing to change even if our partner doesn't, it's a crossroad. That whole concept goes against everything we know and want. It's not a decision to be made lightly.''

I walked to the front window and watched Crystal pull out of our driveway. She turned her car in the direction of her mother's home. I prayed silently that God would intervene in a supernatural way to reconcile her heart back to Him.

Chapter Eleven

Initiate Change

When you live in a temporary residence that is woefully too small for your family, you learn to make accommodations with space and convenience. The next morning, however, I found myself caught in an almost impossible situation. There seemed to be no concessions I could make to solve my dilemma.

Two months before, a charity had asked Pat and me to participate in a fund raising project. Because of Pat's connection with the Orlando Magic basketball team, we were invited to be one of a group of celebrity couples. We were to submit a recipe for the dinner. I knew that my special cheese pie would be a great dessert. We agreed to supply the dessert recipe for the event.

At ten o'clock that morning I got a phone call reminding me that we had agreed to provide dessert for the 500 people who were attending the dinner. I tried to explain that neither Pat nor I had understood that we were to provide the dessert for that many people. Unfortunately, the dinner was the next evening and we were already on the program. There was no way that we could get out of the commitment. I put in an S.O.S. call to Pat's office.

He sympathized but agreed that we couldn't wiggle our way out of the engagement.

I cook for ten hungry mouths three times every day of the week, but cooking a dessert for 500 in my kitchen would be a formidable feat. The oven in our rented house is barely adequate.

I called Crystal to see if she could drop by the house and help. Hoping I would find her at home, instead of at her mother's, I was pleased when she answered the phone. Without any inquiries about Richard's job, I explained my situation and asked if she could help me. It was Crystal's day to work at the church, but she agreed to ask for the time off.

As she was making her way over to our house, I tried with pencil and paper to figure a way out of the situation. How many pans would I need to cook to make 500 portions of cheese pie? How many pans of dessert could I get into my oven at one time? How many hours would it take to prepare and bake all those cheese pies?

When Crystal arrived, we started to figure together. She would go to the people in the neighborhood and church to borrow enough pans. I would run to the store and purchase the ingredients. Almost as an afterthought, Crystal said, "Perhaps we should make a trial run. Let's make one or two recipes of the pie to see how it turns out." Since I had never baked the cheese pie in our rental oven, her suggestion seemed reasonable.

Twice, Pat called to check on our progress and offer his support. Crystal volunteered to go to the store for the vanilla while I measured and stirred the cheese, sugar, and eggs. Before I put the uncooked pie into the oven, I lowered the temperature to the lowest setting because experience had taught me that the calibration was off and everything had to cook at a lower temperature.

As we waited for the sample pie to cook, Crystal and I sat down to talk. "I guess you're wondering what happened yesterday after I left your house."

"Yes, but I wasn't going to ask," I said.

"When I pulled out of your driveway, I was headed for my mother's. However, about halfway there, I was sitting at a red light when suddenly I understood the point that you and Pat were trying to make. You weren't asking me to become a doormat. You were asking me to grow up and take responsibility for my own actions and reactions.

"Of course, you weren't making an unreasonable demand on me. That is the kind of thing I should be doing without a lecture. I knew that my irrational reactions had to stem from the hurts I suffered in the past from my father. Silently, waiting for the light to change, I asked God to help me stop reacting to Richard and initiate the changes that are needed in our marriage.

"Jill, I want Richard to know that he can trust me. I could see that I have constantly been on his back about his job over the past year. At times I'm sure I haven't shown him how proud I am of his accomplishments. I've made him feel that I can't be trusted with his feelings. I don't want to be that way with Richard. I want him to understand that I love him enough that he can come to me with anything that's hurting or disturbing him. How can I show him that I love him?" Crystal asked. We were beginning to smell a delicious, sweet aroma coming from the oven.

I went over to check the cheese pie. As I opened the oven door, I reassured her, "There is nothing mysterious about showing Richard that you are in love. As a couple you are continually teaching each other—giving signals much the way a quarterback motions to his backfield." I closed the oven door, thinking that the pie seemed to be cooking too fast. I tried to lower the temperature, but the oven temperature was already at its lowest setting. I put my misgivings aside, though. This recipe never fails. Nothing could go wrong.

I sat back down at the table and said to Crystal, "If you were ever a part of a sporting team, you learned early that in order to win the game, you have to be able to communicate properly. It's obvious that communication is more than a string of words which make a sentence. A football team with a quarterback who gives a faulty set of signals will tell the opponent what plays are to be used. With the element of surprise eliminated, the margin for winning is automatically narrowed.

"The same is true in a marriage. We are constantly receiving and sending unique signals which only we understand. On occasion, the play is amazingly successful. At other times, we fumble the ball badly. Often the signals we give can have practical applications.

"The other day, I was in the doctor's office with one of the children and there was an old *Business Week* on the reading table. It was a January 1983 issue. As I flipped through the pages, I became interested in an article about women who have become the heads of family businesses. It went into detail about one couple. When they incorporated, the wife became the president and boss. Her husband took the position of vice-president in charge of marketing.

"The article explained that the wife was good at administrative details and a better boss. She was extremely disciplined, while her husband was creative, could meet clients, and keep them happy.

"In their marriage, the husband should be the head, as God prescribes in the Scriptures, but I tried not to be judgmental about their business arrangement. When I looked at it from a noncritical standpoint, I realized that perhaps I could learn from this woman. Had she learned to make her husband so confident in his good points that he could allow her to develop in the areas where she excelled?''

By now, I knew that something awful was happening inside the oven. The horrible smell of burned cheese had reached our nostrils. In a flash, I bolted to the oven. It was too late. The top layer of the cheese pie was black.

At that moment, Pat called. Crystal and I didn't know whether to laugh or cry. There was no way that I could cook the cheese pies in this oven. Because it was approaching lunchtime, Pat offered to come home to help us. I had no idea what he could do, but I jumped at the chance to have someone else here to offer advice in finding a solution. Time was ticking away. With every passing second, Pat and Jill Williams's Magic Cheese Pie for those 500 people who had purchased tickets to eat dessert seemed more and more like the impossible dream.

Crystal and I went to the store near our home to pick up some rolls for our salad lunch. When we got home, Pat was waiting. He had put out the salads and our drinks.

In a few minutes, the conversation drifted from solving the dessert melodrama to Richard and Crystal. I explained to Pat about our morning conversation and how each couple gives signals to each other.

"There are negative signals in a marriage also," Pat said as he dipped into his salad with his fork. "This set of signals can show us if a relationship is fragrant or putrid, thriving or withered.

"There are three deadly signals:

"*Inattentiveness*. When the marriage partners are no longer tending to the store, it doesn't take long before the store goes bankrupt. Not everyone who's physically present is emotionally awake."

Pat shared that we had received a letter from a woman named Joan the other day. Her marriage was dying, and Joan knew it. Joan lamented in her letter, "It wasn't that Jack stayed out nights or went to see other women. Maybe I could have fought that. It was simply that Jack didn't seem to live with me anymore. Sure, he came home and he ate his meals with us and slept in our bed, but he only came alive when he was at work or with one of his fishing buddies."

"Jack, on the other hand," Pat continued, "insisted that he was perfectly happy with his home life. He continued to affirm his marital bliss until one day he met a young woman at the office. She was attractive and 'made him feel alive again.'

"Joan had seen the signals and had tried to arouse her sluggish husband but couldn't. Jack sloughed along until a pretty, young attraction added the spark he insisted wasn't missing.

"*Confidentiality*. Trust can only be built in the atmosphere of confidence. Women are far more apt to talk about confidences with a female confidant than men. Yet men can be guilty as well.

"*Willingness to work*. Relationship and friendship are key words when you are striving to succeed in marriage. Nelson Price, in his book *Tenderness* (Revell, 1986), explains, 'A good relationship is like life insurance: If you need it and you haven't got it, it's too late to get it.' The development of friendship with your spouse should be a lifelong ambition.

" 'A friend is a person with whom your soul can go naked. You don't need to put on anything around a friend. You don't have to be better or worse, just yourself,' continues Price. 'A marriage based on such friendship is not just for better or worse, but for good.'

"Crystal, there must be a resolute determination that a marriage will be a solid, thriving relationship, or the marriage can become an arena for one continuous power struggle.

"H. Norman Wright, director of Christian Marriage Enrichment and Family Counseling and Enrichment, in Santa Ana, California, and author of over fifty books on family and marriage, believes that two of the greatest things that a woman can do for her husband are as follows:

• She can help him to see himself.
• She can help him understand himself.

"There are few women who would disagree with Mr. Wright, but how can a wife accomplish those lofty goals and still maintain harmony within her marriage?

We had finished our salads. "Got any dessert?" Pat asked me in a tease. Then pulling a set of note cards from his briefcase, Pat continued his talk with Crystal.

"One clue is to know what stage of life her husband may be passing through.

"Sally Conway in her book *You and Your Husband's Mid-Life Crisis* (David C. Cook, 1980) points out that 'a lot of time, effort, and money have been spent studying certain phases of life—childhood, adolescence, the senior years, and even women's menopause. But until recently there has been little acknowledgment that there are other stages in adult life.' She goes on to say that recent research provides documented proof that both men and women go through several transition times.

"One of these researchers, Daniel Levinson (*The Seasons of a Man's Life,* Knopf, 1978) writes about the importance to a good marriage of recognizing and reacting positively to the changing stages of life: 'All marital relationships begin with some combination of strengths and problems. A couple is never fully prepared for marriage, no matter how long and how well the partners have known each other. Couples who settle early for a very limited relationship may find this sufficient for a while, but in time the discontents will erupt in gross conflict or will lead to a stagnant marriage. Continuing developmental work is required of individuals and couples in successive periods of the life course.'

"Early in married life, Crystal, a wise woman will put order into her life. She will set priorities. The order should be—Jesus, husband, children, herself, home, outside activities. This is not an easy balance to maintain, and it will take strength," Pat said.

"During this time, a wife's strength must not be like that of a man, but more fluid and movable. Nelson Price explains the kind of courage that must be exhibited. 'When a Western mind thinks of strength, it thinks of steel. The Oriental mind envisions water. Water waits its moment, conforming to the contour of its container. It may wait for years behind a large earthen dam, the configuration of the lake determining its shape. When there is a tiny hole in the dam, the water gently seeps through. As it does, it opens the hole a bit more. It works slowly at first, but eventually it exerts its force and washes away the dam.'

"When a husband sees that you have determined to put his needs and desires first and that there is strength behind that decision, his response will be to love in return.

"As time goes on and a man's responsibilities—financial and otherwise—increase, he is apt to show some signs of dissatisfaction.

"The feelings of this period are hard to pinpoint. A young man confided to his wife, 'Julie, you're everything I've ever wanted in a wife and more; but there's something wrong. I don't know what it is. Like a dull headache, I don't feel sick enough to go to the doctor, but I know I'm not well.'

"During this stage, a man feels the nagging, unconfessed fear that his pain could be the symptoms of a deeply rooted problem. What if all his life choices have been one horrendous mistake? What if he doesn't really love his wife or children but has only been fooling himself and them? What if he could never really love anyone?

"At this stage, the power of words is vital. Gary Smalley and John Trent, Ph.D., teach in *The Blessing,* 'Words have incredible power to build us up or tear us down emotionally. This is particularly true when it comes to giving or gaining family approval.'

"You are now a family, and what you say must be gauged carefully. In order to be helpful,

—Share with Richard what *you* see happening to him, but in a positive way he can handle.

—Never judge or accuse him. Preface your observations about him with, 'I feel . . .' Therefore, you are not making judgments about him but personal observations.

—Don't be a know-it-all. Tell him that you don't have all the answers either, and cite examples of your failures.

—Support and encourage him continually.

—Be willing to help him experiment and find answers.

"No matter how many times you tell yourself, the Lord, and your husband that he is important to you, the time will come when his career and other activities and commitments will threaten to yank you apart.

"This is a crucial time to make sure that any sexual problems which have become more than a gnawing nuisance don't escalate into serious problems. Ed Wheat, M.D., and others have written excellent books on the subject. *Intended for Pleasure* and *Love Life for Every Married Couple* by Dr. Wheat are two examples of many of the Christian books that are available. They will enrich and enliven your love.

You and Richard find yourselves right in the middle of the most famous stage of all—the Seven Year Itch. Although the Seven Year Itch has generally referred to a husband's sudden interest in other women, it apparently has its root cause in the fact that marital satisfaction tends to be low between the seventh and tenth years. A wife has to be alert to danger signs and do her best to spark interest in the marriage.

"Jesus could have been speaking to a wife facing these years of marriage when He said, 'Be as wise as a serpent and as gentle as a dove.' (*See* Matthew 10:16.)

"The pastor of a large congregation admits that for a decade, he thought he had a perfect marriage. One day his wife sat him down and said, 'Dear, you have barked out orders for ten years. I've let you have everything you wanted without question.

" 'My total bending to your will has not drawn us closer together but we are now farther apart than I could've imagined possible. I want you to know that I love you more today than I did when we married; but if something isn't done about our relationship, you will totally destroy me as a person.

" 'You think you know me, but you don't. I've only told you what I knew you wanted to hear. From here on out, you will get my opinion, honestly and truthfully.'

"Tears welled up in her eyes as she said, 'I've prayed for months about this decision, and you must understand that I honestly believe that the action I'm taking is the only thing that will save our marriage.'

"The pastor admits that he was struck dumb but his wife was true to her word. 'Pam didn't nag or argue with me because she isn't that kind of person. Nevertheless, she suddenly came alive.

" 'After my initial negative reaction,' he admits, 'I became fascinated with this new woman I had on my hands. She made increased and exciting demands of me and my time. There was a sense between us that she meant business. Pam is a godly woman. I knew she had heard from God. As I look back on this incident which happened almost twenty years ago, I realize that her decision saved our relationship.'

"Pam read the signals, prayed until God gave her a creative plan of action, and then she acted on it.

" 'A husband's mid-life crisis is going to cause a wife some of the greatest stresses that she has ever experienced,' says Sally

Conway. . . . 'Even though a woman and her husband may have had a fairly stable marriage, the mid-life crisis will surely test it.'

"Crystal, believe me, it's hard to admit that you can't do the things at forty-five that you did at twenty-five. When a man slams nose to nose with that stark reality, he becomes disoriented and confused. That confusion often leads to anger.

"Norman Wright, in an article entitled, 'Your Husband's Mid-life Transition' (*Virtue,* January/February 1988) explains, 'Be patient during this time of adjustment since you may discover your husband is quite changeable. He vacillates greatly in what he wants and what pleases him. So you will find it difficult to meet his needs. This is an unsettled, frustrating time for him! Be resilient!'

" 'The exciting thing both you and your husband need to know' to quote Sally Conway again, 'is that once the mid-life transition has been successfully made, there is a better life ahead. . . . Marriages can become stronger and more satisfying if both of you have "hung in there" during the rough times and have not made the irreparable decision to give up.'

"Bud Earhart is the unofficial elder statesman at Trinity Presbyterian Church. Past seventy years of age, he still keeps active by walking to the church several times a day to check the status of the activities and functions. As church treasurer, his mind is kept alert.

"Most importantly, his spiritual eyes and ears are kept sharp by his relationship with the Lord. During the Christmas of 1987, every member of his family came together. 'I took time to talk with every child and grandchild individually,' Bud shared. 'Even though I felt I knew about the commitments which had been made by each one, I asked them about their relationship with the Lord. We laughed and sang and cried together. I wouldn't take a million dollars for that time.

" 'It was the most satisfying two weeks of my life.' Bud has learned to live every day of his life with enthusiasm. His wife, Ethel, has been his encouragement all along. She helps with love, but she prods and pushes when necessary.

"Crystal, I've gone into great detail to help you understand that the marriage you are struggling with now is like a living organism. It will grow and mature just the way you and Richard do. After the first initial years, you'll face other struggles, but there are great rewards waiting for you.

"When Jill and I urge you to initiate changes in your life, it's because we know that there is a great adventure on the other side of the veil of discouragement you've been living with these last months.

"Much of the oneness you seek with Richard can't be taught, only experienced. Prayerfully watch the signals that Richard, time, and the Lord deal out to you. As you respond with love and understanding to his unique needs, your rewards will build up. For 'the latter things' are often better than 'the former things' and that's especially true in marriage."

After lunch, Pat left for the office and Crystal went back home. I was alone with my burned cheese pie and a vision of 500 hungry mouths to feed. Suddenly I had an inspiration. Jumping to the phone, I called our neighborhood grocery store. They had a deli and facilities to cook pies—lots of pies. "I have a cheese pie recipe that needs to be multiplied. Could you duplicate the recipe for me?"

"Sure, Mrs. Williams." The clerk's voice seemed angelic. "How many does your pie serve?"

"Six."

"How many people do you want to serve?"

"Five hundred." I expected a gulp or some kind of exclamation.

Instead the angelic clerk said in an even voice, "When do you need the pie?"

"By noon tomorrow," I said, hesitant that my deadline would kill even a heavenly deli-man.

"When can you get the recipe to us?" The calmness in his voice was starting to worry me. Maybe he didn't understand what I'd said.

"Did you understand me?" I questioned. "I need cheese pie to serve 500 people by noon tomorrow."

"Mrs. Williams, you are the only customer I ever had who has a family of ten people. You are this store's best patron. You bring the recipe within the hour and I guarantee that you'll have cheese pie to serve 500 people by noon tomorrow."

The Williams's cheese pie was the hit of the charity dinner. Whenever I pass the grocery store, I thank God for them, their angelic clerks, and their big, efficient ovens.

Chapter Twelve

Richard's Turn for Change

With Jill's recent cheese-pie crisis safely behind us, I felt it was time to talk with Richard about the developments of the week. I understood exactly why he would not want to share *unnecessary, trifling* details about his life—like changing jobs—with Crystal.

In the early years of our marriage, I dealt with every situation concerning Jill the same way I'd learned to handle the press. Anyone who has had to maintain a working relationship with a press corps understands the fundamentals.

You are friendly and can even be chatty with them. However, you tell the press only necessary information. They don't need or want to hear everything. In fact, if you give them too much to write about, they can destroy you and your team.

With Jill, I felt that I was protecting her by keeping the grime and grit of my job out of her life. Details were not necessary for her to know. Decisions should be shared only after I had wrestled with them and the final outcome was known.

There was no need for Jill to know when there was a shake-up in the management of the team. She would only become worried and concerned. I felt that part of my position as husband and protector was to be sure that she didn't have to bother her pretty head with unpleasant things that were really none of her business.

My attitude, however, changed 180 degrees in December 1983 when I came to see what my true position as husband meant. I had found that Jill is the greatest confidant I could ever have. Once I took advantage of the opportunities she gave me to open up to her, I found that she could comfort and counsel. Jill instinctively knew when to be stern or quiet. She listened attentively and gave advice sparingly. Gradually, Jill has become a sounding board for all decisions, and her input is invaluable.

I called Richard and arranged to meet him the next day at the racquetball courts. After our first game, we stopped to wipe our faces and have some fresh orange juice. I asked him, "How's your work coming?"

"Great," he lied, examining the dirty sweat he had wiped onto the white gym towel.

"I heard that you've applied for a new position?"

"How did you know about that?"

"Crystal told Jill and me."

"But Crystal doesn't know."

"Richard, I think this could be the time for you to start the next step in our plan. Remember, ANOINT. It's time for you to **Initiate Some Changes.** I completely identify with the position it appears you've taken in this issue. Could it be you have the false assumption that in keeping her in the dark you are protecting her? You and Crystal are one. When you're hurting, she's hurting. When you plan change, she must be a part of the preparation that leads to the change."

Richard took a long drink of orange juice. With the sweatband on his wrist, he removed the excess from his lips and said, "I didn't want Crystal to know that my job is in jeopardy. There are some major shake-ups coming in the construction firm. Two weeks ago the boss called me aside to tell me he is about to merge with another company. It could mean that my entire department would be abolished. I've been put on notice.

"This thing has me scared, Pat. I've worked with this operation since I was in high school. They know my potential. They also know my shortcomings. My boss has nurtured me. He has allowed me to succeed in the areas where I have talent and has taught me how to compensate in the weak spots of my life.

"I could never go to college, but I'm a worker. I have innovative ideas and, just as important, I can put them into practice on the construction site and in the office.

"It never entered my mind that this corporation wouldn't be my home base for the rest of my life. That may seem shortsighted, yet it's been a security for me." I was amazed that Richard confided in me about his job status with that much freedom. It encouraged me that he was ready to begin to share with Crystal.

I tried to hide the excitement in my voice because I understood the heartache he was suffering. Yet, I also realized that this terrible situation could be an oppportunity for him to allow his feelings to be released. Richard was being put in a spot where he would be forced to trust Crystal. "Richard," I said, "you must tell Crystal all that you've told me."

"I can't. Last Sunday when she was pouting, I thought she knew, but how could I tell her that I'm a failure?"

"You aren't a failure. The company may merge and eliminate your position. That doesn't reflect on your character."

"Okay, I know that. You know that. But will Crystal understand?"

"You'll never be sure unless you trust her enough to expose your feelings to her. Richard, you have built a wall of plexiglass around you, but that wall is about to smother your relationship with your wife. You must tell her about your life."

"How? How do I begin?"

"Tonight while you're eating supper, turn off the TV. That's the first step. Then, openly and honestly tell her about the changes that are taking place in the firm and in your position. Third—and this is the most important thing, but it's also the hardest—tell her as much about how you *feel* as you can. If you're scared, she won't think less of you if you tell her that. She'll admire your courage and integrity in letting her be a part of your emotions."

"You're asking for a lot. You want me to expose myself in front of the woman I love. You say I have to risk losing her by telling her my fears."

"You're right. I'm asking you to initiate a change in your life. You are the head of your household. What is the main thing Crystal complains about?"

"That I never share with her or tell her my emotions. But that's just wife talk. She can't really want to know my concerns."

"Now's the time to find out. You'll be surprised how easy it will be and what a tremendous relief you'll experience. There is no doubt in my mind that Crystal has seen those emotions already. You can't be one with a person and not share his or her anxieties.

"Richard, I understand where you are." I reached out to reassure him. "I've lived in your shoes. There have been times in our marriage that I've bottled up huge amounts of emotion and concern. Now, Jill knows every aspect of my life that I'm consciously aware of. She has become my friend. I've come to trust and depend on her advice and wisdom. She knows me the way no other person can. The best part is that, intuitively, she has insights into my character that no one on earth has ever perceived. Together, we're becoming an unbeatable team.

"The word husband has an interesting history. It came from a Norse word, *husbondi*. It's made up of two words: *hus* meaning house and *bondi* meaning holder. The husband is the one who holds the house together. He is the glue of the family. He is the one who puts his arms around the wife and children to hold them into a unit. He is the defender—the guard of the family. As men, we've fouled up the meaning of the word. We are providers for our family. Yet we've not learned how to be their protector. The only thing we protect is our ego.

"The wife in the family is the barometer. She sets the tone and atmosphere of the home. In Proverbs 31, we are told that a wife is to look after the affairs of her household. In your marriage, you've made that impossible for Crystal because she has no idea what is taking place in her husband's life or in her life. You could be without a job in a few days, and she's not even supposed to be aware of that.

"When Crystal is sensing by your actions that there is an atmospheric disturbance, and you refuse to tell her, you disregard her emotions and make her feel insecure and vulnerable.

"When you start to share openly with Crystal, that will be a demonstration of love that will overwhelm her."

We continued to play until our time ran out on the courts. We showered and changed clothes and the conversation gradually shifted to the Super Bowl. As we prepared to leave, Richard stopped and said, "Pat, I know you're right. This will be the hardest night of my life, but I'm going to tell Crystal about the merger. Pray I don't blow it."

"You won't flub it, Richard. Crystal will help you. She knows more about you than you can imagine. She'll make it easy."

"You may be right, but I know one thing. Whether she understands or not, I feel as though I've just left a fifty pound weight on that racquetball court. I guess being a self-made man isn't as appealing as the impression we were given when we were growing into adults."

I patted Richard's back to encourage him. "You are about to embark on one of the greatest adventures in your life. Paul tells us to love our wives just as Christ loved the Church and gave Himself for her.

"My love for Jill is to be costly and active. A token of my love—a new car, a paycheck, even human emotion—won't do. The marital love Paul talked about is active, costly service. By learning to lay aside my own personal desire and ambitions to meet her needs, I am becoming what God desires for me.

"When I think of the amazing privilege we have to become like Christ in this tangible way, I can hardly contain my excitement and expectation.

"Be careful not to approach Crystal with a loud or abrasive attitude, either. Colossians 3:19 (NIV) says, 'Husbands, love your wives and do not be harsh with them.' As men, we find ourselves with a problem. Howard Hendricks calls it an ''omni-science complex.'' In other words, we think that men know more than women and that we are more logical, more competent, and more capable. That perspective makes us quick to blurt out easy answers and slow to hear. The result is a harshness that destroys a women's self-esteem.

"I hate to admit it, Richard, but one of the hardest things I have ever had to do was learn to listen to Jill. After all, to my overinflated ego, it meant the sacrifice of my great wisdom and my superior opinions. Fran Sciacca said, 'Learning to listen to my wife is as hard for me as pushing a chain.'

"Yet marriage is the most mutually rewarding and fulfilling adventure God has given to man. By listening to Crystal, you will be building her self-confidence and your happiness at the same time."

We headed for opposite ends of the parking lot where our cars were parked. In my excitement, I lost all my suave maturity and turned and yelled like a schoolboy, "Call to tell me about the outcome." Richard's apprehension showed on his face. I hoped that my excitement would bolster his resolve to become honest with Crystal.

Chapter Thirteen

Who Is This Stranger I Sleep With?

Until a child graduates from high school, his parents experience all four seasons of the year: football season, basketball season, baseball season, soccer season. Of course, even a mother knows the year does not begin in January. That's the month you're waiting for the Super Bowl results and the end of the pro football season. The year actually commences in September with the first football practice.

The second season (basketball) of the 1987–88 year was almost a memory, and baseball practice was about to start. One afternoon I took Michael over to check on the progress of the addition to our house. We go every day to pick up the mail, answer questions about the plans, and see where each new nail has been placed.

Unfortunately, none of us had thought to prepare three-year-old Michael for the construction progress that had been made the previous day. As we walked hand-in-hand into the backyard, dodging boards and rusty nails, Michael suddenly released a

blood-curdling scream. "My pool. They broke my pool. I want
my pool." After his initial shock, Michael dissolved into tears.

Where our backyard pool had once been, there was now a fresh
pile of black dirt. I stooped down and held Michael in my arms,
trying to console him. "They covered your pool with dirt, but the
men are going to dig us a new one. It will be in another place in
the yard, and it will be larger, newer, and more beautiful."

Michael refused to be comforted and continued to sob. He had
become the favorite of all the men who were working on the
house. When they heard his scream, work was suspended, and
they came down from the rafters and the roof to see what had
happened to their little friend.

When I told Pat about the incident, he immediately related it to
some of the hurts I'd experienced in our early marriage because
he had not been able or willing to communicate with me. I would
be happily building my life when suddenly I'd discover Pat had
filled my pool up with dirt.

This pattern was repeated so frequently in our lives that I
eventually refused to believe that things would ever be rectified,
because my heart had been deeply wounded. "There are a lot of
tears which can be avoided by talking with each other," Pat said
in a plaintive tone.

"You still don't like the way I share all the details about
events."

"That's true, but this incident with Michael and the pool
reiterates your viewpoint that details can be important."

"I hope Crystal has not been so hurt by Richard's inability to
share about the firm's merger that she will have a rough time
forgiving him," I said. After Pat had repented, I couldn't believe
him for months. The miserable times flashed into my mind. I
couldn't respond to him. Like Michael, my emotions had taken
control of my brain and no amount of coaxing could change the
facts as I saw them.

The next morning as I turned the corner of the street and
headed for our house, my concerns about Crystal were erased.
Her car was behind me. She was waving and blowing her horn.
I pulled over to the side of the road. She bounced out of her car

and asked, "Are you going to be home this morning? I have to talk with somebody." The excitement in her eyes was more eloquent than poetry.

Coincidentally, Pat and Richard had accidentally run into each other at the grocery store, and Richard had given Pat a glowing report of the events of the night before.

Richard had come in and, as usual, had turned on the TV to watch the news, but when dinner was served, he turned off the set. Crystal was shocked and thought that he was about to reprimand her about the children's behavior or some other thing. "No," he said smiling. "I thought we might talk for a change."

"Pat, I don't know why, because it isn't our custom, but when we gave thanks for the meal, I reached over and took Crystal's hand. With that tiny gesture, it was as though a volcano of joy erupted inside of her. I don't think I've ever seen her that happy. I'm not sure what the next chapter is. I caught a sneak preview of the great adventure you were talking about the last time we met.

"By the time I had finished explaining to her about the merger of the firm, she had made me feel like I could conquer the world. I listened to her, and the things she said made good sense. Crystal came up with an excellent suggestion.

"The corporation we will merge with is known for working with the handicapped. However, there have been some major problems with assimilation of these employees. Crystal thought I should propose a plan to form a separate division in which the handicapped could be acclimated gradually into their new posts. Many established employees, in turn, need to be educated on how to interface with the handicapped. I could form the division and set the needed programs into motion.

"It would be a totally new experience for me, but that's the kind of challenge I thrive on. Because of my learning disabilities, I can understand the struggles of being handicapped. Though I've worked hard to cover my problems, there is an empathy which comes through shared sorrow," Richard said.

Meanwhile, Crystal had arrived at our house to talk to me. It was hard to imagine that the radiant young woman who shared with me that morning was the same person who only a few months before had been at the crossroads of despair.

"Many nights as I lay in bed after making love to Richard, I've asked myself, 'Who is this stranger who is sleeping with me?' " Crystal admitted. "Last night, for the first time since we were dating, I saw the man I married. Richard is concerned about his position with the company, of course, but the Lord has always provided for us.

"While we were talking, I could see Richard working with the handicapped. I had no idea that the corporation that is merging with Richard's company is known all over the country for hiring the handicapped. But there have been major problems. When I told Richard about what I saw, he became excited. Within twenty minutes, we had come up with a proposal in which Richard could play a vital part in the new corporation. Of course, he will have to sell the idea to the new corporate board, but Richard has always been more convincing than a howling snowstorm."

"Crystal," I said, "this is a major step. Soon you will put into practice all the steps in the ANOINT plan."

"Jill, I'm ahead of you. The next part of ANOINT is **Notice His Needs.** There is only one thing that Richard repeatedly says he needs from me, and that's a good sexual relationship. That may sound unspiritual, but it's true."

I nodded in agreement. "If more men and women were honest, they would say that sex is an overriding need of most men in marriage. I'm sure that psychologists know why that is true.

"I don't have any statistics or figures, but I know that wherever Pat and I go to speak, most women tell me that sex is the area in which they feel least able to satisfy their husbands. So I know that you aren't alone in your struggle."

"As we lay in bed last night," Crystal said, "I looked at Richard. We had made love, and he was sound asleep. I watched the rhythmic breathing movements of his body, and I asked God to help me to become the marriage partner he desires me to be."

"Crystal, that was a monumental decision. A wise missionary who had spent twenty-five years in the heart of Brazil was teaching a Bible class years ago. She said, 'Whether you are in the jungles of Brazil or the sophisticated suburbs of Chicago, a marriage is made or broken in the bedroom.' I was young and didn't understand the full implication of what she said, but that phrase stuck with me.

"Over the years, I've learned some important things through observation. One of the largest contributors to marriage problems is sexual incompatibility. However, less than 2 percent of sexual incompatibility is physical. The other 98 percent is a mental attitude.

"I'm sure that you realize God never intended sex to be merely a union. It is designed to be communion. For that reason, sexual activity should always be preceded by and involve acts of love. With the hurried schedules of the modern woman, we can develop the attitude of having sex in a hurry to merely get it behind us for the day. It can become another thing to check off our list in our quest to be the perfect Christian woman. Of course, at first, you don't intend to drop the important foreplay which leads to intercourse. But one day you wake up and realize that your sex life is all sex and no love."

Crystal was listening intently. There was a long pause in the conversation as I went to the refrigerator to get us a fresh glass of grapefruit juice. Finally, she said, "Jill, I'm embarrassed and offended because Richard is almost an animal in bed. He appears to have no self-control."

I poured another glass of juice and sat down. "Don't make the mistake of judging your husband's sexual needs by your own. Men are sexual creatures. There is an actual physical need for him to have an orgasm, and no amount of prayer or fasting is going to relieve that need.

"If you are offended by his need for release, it communicates rejection to him. As wives, the way we respond to our husband's sexual needs either builds up or rips apart his self-image. When we reject, tolerate, or resist his initiation of sex, we are communicating that we are rejecting him as a person."

"But that's not true. I love Richard."

"The other night Pat shared with me from a book he was reading by Jill Renich, *To Have and To Hold*. She states that for a man, 'Sex is the most meaningful demonstration of love and self-worth. It is part of his own deepest person.'

"Men are shown through the media as always assertive and sexually competent. The truth is that when a man is faced with the real-life struggles of being a husband, he is not always in total control. In fact, many men suffer from acute fear. He is concerned about three basic things in his sex life:

"He wonders whether his wife is enjoying sex. In your conversations, you should reassure him of your unconditional acceptance of him. Though he may try to hide his need for verbal assurances, Richard desires to be told that he is a wonderfully satisfying lover. Tell him you enjoy his body, and reassure him that the imperfections don't matter to you.

"He fears he may lose the ability to continue to perform. The locker-room jokes about losing his ability to make love will come back to haunt him. The spectre appears during the oddest times. This fear is a sign of low self-confidence. Many men feel that if they lose their ability to make love to their wives, they will also lose her self-respect as well. While this isn't true, the fear exists and should not be ignored.

"He fears losing his ability to satisfy her. You need to openly tell Richard what your needs are. Be willing to listen to his suggestions about changes you can make. When you share your fears, worries, and problems, he will be understand that you are also searching for a better relationship. Jill Renich wrote, 'To receive him with joy and to share sexual pleasure builds into him a sense of being worthy, desirable, and acceptable.' "

I shared with Crystal a quote from Dennis and Barbara Rainey. They have said, "Great sacrifice communicates great love. Freely giving of yourself to your mate will make you a magnet to him, drawing him home, keeping him safe. The wife who really loves her husband will choose to take risks to please her man.

"To please your husband sexually is to build his sense of value as a man. He will feel needed, fulfilled, and confident. He will experience the protection that marriage was intended to provide from the temptations of the world.

"Crystal, last summer we spent some time at a Christian camp where Pat and I were speaking. One afternoon the head of the campgrounds joined us by the pool. A seasoned minister who has seen thousands of families come through the camp, he said, "Pat, I wish you could convey the message to women that the greatest ministry a wife can have is to meet her husband's sexual needs."

"Crystal, that thought has absolutely revolutionized my attitude toward the act of marriage. It was as though a firecracker had exploded inside me. Could satisfying his sexual needs be part of my *ministry* to Pat?

"It seemed so clear that I couldn't believe that I'd missed this vital part of our life. Have you ever noticed how often women complain that they don't know what God's will for their lives is? We want a *ministry*. Well, God has given us His will for ministry to our husbands. Now we need to obey."

By the time Crystal left, it was noon. Pat surprised me by coming home for a few hours in the afternoon. Michael went to bed for a nap. As the house grew quiet, Pat and I sat on the couch in the living room. "I hope I don't appear to be the kind of person who has all the answers when I'm sharing with Crystal," I said to Pat. "Because as she and I talked this morning, I was made aware of my own shortcomings. There is really no way that we can help each other without God's supernatural intervention. All I can do is to ask for wisdom from God, again and again, whenever Crystal and I are together."

Pat took my hand and said, "Perhaps the most underrated, yet valuable, tool God has given to mankind is wisdom. In addition, the Lord pours it out to us whenever we ask, and He never scolds us for asking. Remember, James 1:5 (NAS) says, 'But if any of you lacks wisdom, let him ask of God, who gives to all men generously and without reproach, and it will be given to him.' "

Pat pulled a small stack of cards from his briefcase and shared a quote that was written on one of them. The Greek mathematician Archimedes said that if he had a fulcrum—the point or support on which a lever turns—he could move the earth. However, Archimedes looked in vain for the fulcrum that would have given him the leverage he needed.

"We're fortunate," Pat said, still holding my hand. "We know what our fulcrum is. God has given wisdom to provide the leverage needed to move the earth."

"Pat, I've noticed that rather than depending on God's wisdom, many women use purely emotional leverage on their husbands."

As we thought and discussed for a few moments, Pat and I sifted the emotional levers used by all marriage partners down to four: anger, romantic love, guilt, fear. As the afternoon sun poured in the living room windows, we couldn't help but marvel at the pressure husbands and wives exert with these tools of human power and influence.

Fear

Within themselves, none of these emotions are sinful. In fact, it is the fear of being killed by a car that keeps a child out of the middle of the highway.

Pat and I were having lunch with a college senior and her parents a few months ago. The student related to us, "AIDS has produced a totally different morality on campus. Casual sex is a thing of the past. Only three years ago, when I was a freshman, it was nothing for a person to have sex with two or three people in one week. No more." The fear of dying of AIDS has done more to reestablish morality than all the sermons of our most noted evangelists.

Yet, fear used as leverage to gain control over a person will only defeat, confuse, and paralyze. The Bible says fear has torment. It can be a most destructive emotion.

I remembered and shared with Pat the story of a family friend I had known while growing up. Marge lived in terror of her alcoholic husband. During several drunken bouts he had threatened to kill the entire family and then turn his gun on himself. Fearing for her life, Marge hid the guns in a small closet which her husband had never used. They were safely hidden for two weeks. Then one night after he had been drinking all day, she heard him stumbling down the hall, mumbling to himself.

Fearing the worst, Marge followed him and found him with his hands in the closet, reaching for the shotgun. "I told you I'd kill you!" he mumbled in a drunken stupor. In terror, she bolted out the door. The two older children saw her flight and took out after her. The youngest child was sleeping in the bedroom next to the closet where the guns were hidden. Marge had totally forgotten him in her terrorized flight from the house.

Once outside, she didn't dare go back in. Fear had caused her to forget her own child as she fled for her life. Finally, the police were called; they entered the house. Her husband feigned total innocence and accused her of overreacting.

"Fear is usually not that blatant, however," Pat said. "One can use fear of disapproval or embarrassment to maneuver a mate, even though that tactic never produces pure or lasting fruit."

Romantic Love

Romantic love can be the greatest joy shared by two people, but this generation has grown up with a distorted, and even perverted, concept of romantic love.

We are programmed to confuse real love with infatuation, while the Cinderella complex runs rampant in every spectrum of society. We are taught in our stories and fantasies that we should expect to live happily ever after. Unfortunately, there is no ideal marriage.

Jack Green, a Baptist preacher from Birmingham, Alabama, once said that there is no such thing as two people who are compatible. They come from different backgrounds. They have different parents and families. They sit on opposite sides of the table. They sleep on opposite sides of the bed.

Of course, that doesn't mean no marriage can be happy. It means that every marriage will involve work. Unfortunately, we aren't taught that "marriage-work" reaps far more blessings than any other human effort. We must fight to keep romance alive in our marriage, but we must also realize that romance isn't the panacea that ends every moment of heartache.

Keeping their relationship a priority had been a determining factor within the marriage of Robert and June Hendricks, a couple we've met since moving to Florida. They often couldn't afford a night out at a restaurant, so they took Sunday afternoon walks in the park near their house. June would take a blanket, and Robert would carry a small thermos with iced tea or coffee. They'd sit and talk for hours, feeding the ducks and holding hands.

One night they were awakened by a knock at the door. A police officer stood inside the lighted hallway. Pain and concern etched his face. Their son, who was only fourteen years old, had been picked up by the officer. He was high on some kind of drug and hallucinating.

Their son had to be hospitalized. Over the next few days, the frightened couple pieced together horrible, unbelievable facts. Their son had been sneaking from the house every night after the rest of the family was in bed. He and several friends would rendezvous on a vacant lot, smoke pot, or experiment with harder drugs. After an hour or more, he would crawl back through his window and sleep off the effects of the drugs.

No words can describe the horror of those next few weeks as this committed Christian couple cried, prayed, and examined every inch of their lives. There were no Sunday afternoon picnics for many months, only lots of nights spent in agonizing analysis.

That was ten years ago. Robert and Joan now realize that those months of anguish and horror bonded them into a closely woven unit. All their candlelit dinners and romantic times had prepared their relationship to endure the heartache, but it was the moments of uncertainty that fused them into a working organism. "But those were horrible months. There were days when I thought Robert and I would tear each other apart as we desperately worked at piecing our family back together," Joan told Pat and me.

"Pat, I wanted romance to cure all my ills," I said, staring at a bluejay which had lit on a bush near the window. "You have become everything I could want in a husband."

"But I pray that God's love will overtake where romantic love leaves off," Pat said.

". . . and I thank God that He has shown us the danger of depending on romance for the total package in our marriage."

Anger

Not everything termed anger is sin, either. Ephesians 4:26 teaches us to "be angry and sin not." However, anger that is used to manipulate or control a situation or another person is sin.

A wife who pouts and withholds sex because her husband forgot to take out the garbage is in sin. The husband who walks into the home and demands that every family member pay homage to his outbursts of rage is in sin.

Guilt

The conscience has been given as a guide by which the Holy Spirit influences us onto the paths He desires us to follow. Paul, speaking in Romans 2:14 (PHILLIPS), gives this perspective. "When the gentiles, who have no knowledge of the Law, act in accordance with it by the light of nature, they show that they have a law in themselves, for they demonstrate the effect of a law operating in their own hearts. Their own consciences endorse the existence of such a law, for there is something which condemns or excuses their actions."

Guilt, when used to get our own way, is the easiest emotional weapon on the market. Each person has his own inner code of conduct. When that code is violated, guilt is produced.

When a mate uses destructive condemnation to get his or her desires, he is playing a dangerous game of Russian roulette. Hospitals for the emotionally disturbed are filled with people who have reached their brink of endurance in self-condemnation. When they are no longer able to meet their own expectations, the mind and emotions break down.

"As destructive as emotional warfare can be," Pat said, "thank God, He has given us a key that can unlock doors of opportunity. That key is wisdom. Because we're told again and again to ask for it, I wonder if wisdom is like Vitamin B. It can't be stored in our spiritual bodies. We need a new supply every day. It appears that wisdom is given, as we need it, in bite-size portions—not by the bushel basket," Pat said, laughing as he got up to return to the office.

I had a few minutes before Michael awakened from his nap and we had to pick up the other children. I used the stillness of those minutes to pray for God's wisdom again.

I asked God to help me remember the facts and common sense that the Lord had helped me share with Crystal. I asked that He would allow a new sacrifice of love to be communicated to Pat through me—not with the emotional tools at my command but with the wisdom that's given freely and liberally whenever we ask.

Chapter Fourteen

Notice Your Partner's Needs

Late that afternoon, I received a phone call from Richard. "Pat, could you and Jill pray for my parents? Crystal and I have to go to Atlanta. My parents live there. There are some business matters that I need to discuss with them. We should be home in a day or two. The girls have two days off from school."

It was a week before Crystal and Richard returned, however. The day after they came back was a Saturday. Richard and I decided to jog together that morning. Normally, I jealously reserve my running time to memorize Scripture. Yet, I sensed that Richard had a special need to talk.

After our three-mile course, we stopped by my house for some juice before Richard ran back home. The morning had been refreshingly cool. A misty fog bathed our faces and bodies as we ran. Both of us seemed to sense that God wanted to do a special work that morning.

I asked Richard about his trip to see his parents. While no tears formed in his eyes, Richard's voice had a mellow and gentle tone which told me that deep emotions had been stirred by his visit. "My parents are remarkable people. I've always known that, but this last trip to see them sealed my admiration for them. We lived in Orlando most of my life. After I graduated from high school, Dad was offered a position in Atlanta. It was a large promotion, and my parents couldn't resist.

"Now it appears that they may need to move back to Florida. Both of them are resisting the relocation. They're afraid that they might be a burden on us, but Crystal and I want them to return."

An awkward silence fell between us. It appeared that Richard assumed that I knew why his parents would have to come back to Florida. I asked him, "Are your parents having financial problems?"

"Yes and no. My father had a heart attack six months ago. He may never be able to return to work. He had only a few years until retirement, but this could hasten it.

"After his hospitalization, Dad was left strangely disabled. He became so weakened that he couldn't even hold a pen or pencil. His mind was no longer clear, and the strain of figures confused and frustrated him. He and my mother had always felt that the finances were his concern. Now Mom is faced with the fact that she has to handle all the bills.

"When I was home, my mom explained that his ability to handle the banking had been a most important responsibility to Dad. He was probably a frustrated accountant at heart and loved to keep elaborate journals and ledgers. He kept an accurate accounting of all their financial concerns. Much time and prayer was poured into knowing how God wanted them to distribute the money they earned.

"For the past ten years, Mother has been a columnist for a newspaper in one of the towns on the outskirts of Atlanta. While Dad respected her prerogative to her paycheck, he was the one who kept the records and paid the bills.

"When Dad became disabled, Mom needed a great deal of wisdom to pay the expenses and still leave Dad's self-respect intact. She has wrestled with this situation all these months. Finally, the Lord showed her last month that Dad was not in control of their lives and she was not in control of their finances. Jesus was in control.

"Once Mother realized that God was not going to let her down and did not want Dad's self-respect harmed, she had peace. Now she and Dad discuss what should be paid. Mom has Dad make up a list of the checks which need to be written, and then she writes out the drafts. By continuing to keep Dad an active part of the process, we have all seen him gaining back his old confidence and self-worth.

"This past week, there were some important decisions to be made about selling their home. For the first time in our lives, Dad wanted his children's advice and opinion. Pat, I'll be honest with you. When Mother called and said that Dad wanted us to come up and discuss some financial matters, I thought he must be on his deathbed. Actually, the opposite had happened. He has grown to see that asking for help doesn't mean that you lose control.

"This was a special time for me. Dad, Mother, Crystal, and I sat down and discussed things. They listened to me. I could tell from their expressions that they value my opinion concerning business decisions." His voice became thin, and I could almost see him trying to maintain control. "My father has been a wonderful man, but until this week, I was only his son. Now, I'm his friend."

At that moment, Jill came into the kitchen and asked if we would like her to fix us some breakfast. "I have an even better idea," I said. "You call Crystal. See if she and the girls can come over for breakfast. Richard and I can take the car and get some wheat muffins and egg sandwiches from the local diner down the street."

Within twenty minutes, Jill and Crystal had set the table with napkins and orange juice. Andrea had put some fresh-cut flowers in the center of the tablecloth. Richard and I bought enough sandwiches to feed a small army.

After our impromptu feast, the boys scattered outside to practice basketball. Two of the girls had household chores to finish, and Karyn practiced her piano. Crystal, Richard, Jill, and I stayed at the table, talking for another hour. Crystal filled Jill in on all the intricate details of their drive to Atlanta. Richard and I listened for a few minutes, then drifted into a conversation of our own.

Something Richard had said in passing this morning had fascinated me. "It was important to you that your parents were interested in your opinions about business?" I asked. "This might seem like an intrusion, but could you tell me how you felt?"

"Sure. The afternoon we left, the freeway was clogged because of the weather, and we were stuck on the road for hours. I had time to think about my feelings.

"While we were in the middle of our discussion, and Dad was asking me for advice about selling their house and tax advantages, I didn't realize their confidence in me was having any impact. It was as though it was a normal conversation between four adults. But during those hours waiting for the traffic to unclog, I was able to reflect on a strange new sensation I was feeling. Crystal and I talked about it, and with her help, I could see that their confidence in me has given me a new assurance of myself and my abilities.

"Of course, it couldn't have come at a better time. With the merger of our company, I need this added boost to help me sell the plan I want to incorporate. Pat, I feel as though I've grown a foot taller. Isn't it odd that having someone value your opinion could make that much difference?"

By now, Crystal and Jill had rejoined us in the conversation. "I can notice a difference in Richard, can't you?" Crystal asked Jill.

Jill laughed. "I thought something great had happened when I first saw him. There is a new confidence. But . . ."

"But, what?" I asked.

"Nothing," she said. "It's the same thing you and I have talked about over and over again."

By now, I've grown attuned to the wistful look which had come into Jill's eyes, and I thought I knew what she was hesitant to say. I reached over and gently rubbed her back. "I believe I know what you're thinking," I said. "You're thinking about all the times that women's opinions are overlooked or totally rejected by their husbands and families only because they are women.''

"True. But it isn't that by itself. Most men reject women's opinions as though we're mindless children. In remodeling our house . . . Pat, you know how many times I've come home frustrated because the workmen won't listen to me. I'll tell them I want the lights for the living room recessed and they ask, 'What does your husband think?' ''

The day before, a conflict had occurred on the job site between one of the workmen and Jill over the way she wanted the kitchen cabinets installed. The incident had left Jill frustrated and angry.

"Jill isn't the only woman to face that attitude, either," Crystal added. "I have taken the car to have it repaired. The mechanic will ask what's wrong. If I act like a fluggle head who doesn't know a carburetor from a gas gauge, I'm patronized but treated nicely—kind of like a lost puppy.

"However, if I tell them that I believe there is water in the gas tank or the power steering fluid seems to be low, or there's condensation in the distributor cap, the mechanic will laugh in my face and say with disgust, 'Yea, we'll see, lady.' ''

Jill, Crystal, and I laughed at her illustration, but Richard looked her straight in the eye. "I haven't treated you much better than that, have I?" While he stumbled over the words, his voice was tender and vulnerable. His expression of deep concern for Crystal caught all of us off guard. Crystal smiled, but her eyes filled with hurts from the past. She looked away from Richard's face.

"Pat, what makes men treat women this way? Even worse, what makes a husband treat his wife with such ego-robbing tactics?"

The atmosphere of the room had turned from festivity to solemnity as we discussed these deeply personal areas of vulnerability and concern. We could almost touch the Holy Spirit. Before I answered, I prayed that God would give me wisdom. I felt that God had plowed up Richard's heart through the acceptance he had gained from his parents. At last he was ready to hear about the hurts Crystal had experienced through his lack of confidence in her. The hardness that had dominated Richard's personality had melted away. He was seeking answers with the openness of a small child.

"I believe we treat our wives with a lack of respect because we have an overwhelming fear of losing control," I said.

"Of course, if you really look at the situation in the light of truth, it's an unfounded fear. God has made man head of the household. This wasn't Adam's or Abraham's idea; the sovereign Lord of the universe devised the plan. Obviously, God gave some added spark to a man's makeup which makes him uniquely capable of handling the responsibility.

"Years ago, I read a statement by Larry Christenson (*The Christian Family,* Bethany Fellowship, 1970): 'Stronger shoulders are given to the man; he has a greater natural strength of mind to enable him to stand up under the pressure of these cares. The heart of a woman is more easily discouraged and dejected.'

"Because we're human—as men—we forget that God's greatest concern is still for individual needs. He is not task oriented. God is not as concerned about who does a specific job, as much as He is about the attitude of the heart. In studying and reading about marriage, I've seen that there are a few marriage counselors and authors of books on the family who firmly believe that a good marriage divides the tasks of life into two separate and uncrossable camps.

"There are the men's duties on the right side, and then there are the women's responsibilities on the opposite page of the ledger. Asserting that 'Divine Order' dictates which job belongs to which spouse, everything is neatly wrapped in a package marked, 'Authority and Responsibility.' "

"We're also trained from childhood to be task oriented in our marriages," Jill added. "In the household in which I was raised, my father, also, handled the checkbook and finances." Jill motioned to Richard. "As a young single woman, I remember my mother and father going over the household accounts. Dad was always the strong leader with the expenses. I felt that it was a large part of the husband's responsibility to pay all the bills. A wife shouldn't have to worry about the utility payments or make sure that the dentist bills were paid.''

"On the other side of town. . . ,'' I took Jill's cue and interjected, "I was the proverbial hassled bachelor. For me, one of the biggest drawbacks of being an unmarried man was having to meet the deadlines of those monthly payments.

"Writing checks was not my idea of a thrilling way to spend an evening. I couldn't wait until I married and turned the task of bill paying over to my deeply devoted spouse. In the first month of our marriage, I presented the checkbook to Jill with the assumption that she would be delighted.'' Jill and I smiled at each other. This had been a large breach in our relationship which has now been healed.

Jill continued the narrative. "Pat's assumption was wrong. He was the head of the house, and in my mind, paying the bills was part of his job description. For many years, it was an area of contention and frustration in my mind.''

"However,'' I added, "most of the arguments about headship that center around task orientation are mute. While God has given us a free will, He has also set certain laws in place. It's commonly asserted that when a woman takes on certain responsibilities, she takes the reigns of headship away from her husband.

"Trying to figure out who is the head of a certain marriage is as silly as trying to figure out who is the president of the United States. We have an elected official as president. He may be an outstanding leader and maintain peace and order, or he may be incompetent, allowing anarchy to reign. But once elected, he is president.

"In fact, the president can delegate most or even all of the responsibilities of his office to someone else. If his wife is influential, he may delegate much of the decision-making process to her, but that does not make her the president. This man, good or bad, will remain our president until his term runs out, he dies, is mentally handicapped, or is impeached.

"God has chosen headship for our families. The Scriptures don't say that the man is the head of the house if he chooses to be, or if his wife will allow him, or if he does all the proper masculine tasks.''

"It would make things a lot simpler for wives," Jill added, "if husbands understood that God has ordained headship to be placed on the man. A wife may choose to respect and submit to that headship or not, but her decisions don't change God's order in the home.''

"If we could disregard circumstances and custom in our marriages, the way your parents did this week, and realize this divine principle, married couples could be free to find God's wisdom as to who is best to perform which tasks," I said.

"Pat is wonderful about putting the children to bed," Jill said. "Every night after supper, he gets up from the table and helps the children with their baths and washing their hair. Even when Sarah and Andrea were tiny and had long, thick oriental locks, he dried and brushed their hair before tucking them into their beds.

"Pat prays with them and for them and spends a few minutes with each child. That's their special time. Washing and drying three little girls' hair each night may not seem like a 'manly' thing to do, but for the past four years God has released us to be who we are.''

A little embarrassed by her praise, I added, "Jill has chosen to remain at home with the children. As a family, we've reaped the benefits in an orderly home life. Once she got over her shock of being handed the checkbook, Jill started to take the management of our material goods to heart. Economy, thrift, and faithfulness are a part of our home.

"No one would ever accuse Jill of being stingy. Yet, when she opens a new stick of butter, Jill automatically scrapes the small excesses which cling to the wrapper and smooths them on to the large bar. This is a small thing, but those tiny measures add large dividends.''

Crystal's interest was sparked. "All right. Tell me. What are some of the things that Jill does that makes the home orderly and happy? Jill is not *Matilda Milquetoast*. I've seen her stand up to you, Pat, and give you her opinion. What makes the difference?''

For a few seconds, I was caught off guard by Crystal's question about specifics. Quickly, however, I gathered in my mind areas where Jill had instinctively known my need to take headship within the family and had pushed to make me secure. I've been comfortable in the security which comes from knowing that I am trusted as the head of the household.

"There are three areas that Jill emphasizes within our relationship that assure me that she is not attempting to usurp my authority," I said. "They give us both great freedom.

"First, *Jill allows me to help her.*

"This may not seem important, but I have repeatedly seen women who complain that their husbands would not help with the household chores. When the poor, bedraggled man finally gave in, however, he was met with continuous criticism. His wife subconsciously or consciously sabotaged every attempt he made to be useful."

"Remember Joyce?" Jill asked me. "She's a young divorcée who became furious every time her ex-husband came to take their two girls for the weekend. Joyce set her children up to resist every advance of affection their father made toward them. With horror stories about other men and subtle implications, their mother destroyed the children's affection for their father.

"Soon their dad gave up the weekend visits. 'I can't handle the girls. It's too painful for me,' he confessed. His time with the children was reduced to a short dinner at a local fast-food restaurant twice a month.

" 'The girls need their father,' Joyce now moans continually. 'How will they ever learn to relate to a man if he won't take time with them? Can you imagine that he tells me that he can't handle the girls? I've had them for four years. How does he think I manage?' "

Jill continued, "I've seen happy Christian homes where wives actually want their husbands to fail with domestic tasks. They relish the idea that their man could never master the complexities of the washing machine. A gleam twinkles in their eyes when they explain, 'Why, he can't even use the microwave.' "

"I'm confident that my contributions are wanted and needed," I said. "While I may not do the task with the same skill and dispatch that Jill does it, she never criticizes me. She is helpful to me when I'm in a trouble spot, without making me the brunt of domestic humor. Therefore, I enjoy doing things for Jill because she is able to accept my help graciously.

"Second, *Jill honestly believes that I have gifts, talents, and resources that she needs within our home.* She will tell anyone that the reason I put the children to bed each night is because I'm better at it than she is.

"I'm not sure when we first realized that this was a unique talent that God had given me, but as our family has mushroomed, I've gravitated to this because I wanted and needed my time with the children.

"We slowly hit upon our nighttime routine because I was free from the work details. After supper, Jill had the older children doing their final chores and homework. I took the younger children in tow and supervised the melee in the back part of the house. Soon we noticed that there was a calming effect on the whole household because of my participation.

"Third, *Jill encourages my ideas and input.* As a bachelor in Chicago I had friends named Willie and Sylvia. I went to their house occasionally for supper. Willie was always encouraged by his wife, Sylvia, to help with the chores around the house. The only hitch was that everything had to be done her way. Sylvia gave lip service to Willie's helpfulness, but if he ever veered from her established plan of action he was in for fireworks.

"That became apparent one evening after a small dinner party. There were probably four couples at their home for dinner. Willie stood up and started stacking the dishes. Sylvia smiled sweetly, 'I've told you a million times, Willie. You should never stack the dishes when you take them from the table.' Their guests were painfully embarrassed.

"Sheepishly, Willie looked at her. 'I find it's easier to take all the dishes at one time instead of two of them.' Then with a feeble attempt to hide his humiliation with humor, he added, 'Guess it's because my hands are bigger.'

" 'I guess it's because you don't have to do the dishes. It

makes my job easier when you do it my way.' With that closing statement, Sylvia ended the conversation.

"Jill not only encourages my ideas but she promotes them. It was my idea that we share our devotions together. Jill never countered my suggestion with a better one. She was willing for me to take the lead and to continue with my hands on the steering wheel. My devotions have always been an area in my life that is important. I love to study and meditate on the Scriptures. That joy has been heightened by my being able to share this time with Jill.

"When we first started studying together, I was hesitant that perhaps I was making demands on Jill. She, however, never gave me any indication that I was being pushy. As I look back, I think that perhaps I could've been more subtle in my enthusiasm to share my 'great wisdom' and biblical knowledge. Yet Jill was interested and happy to become a part of this area of my private life."

"Pat has not stifled me, however, by not allowing me to tell him about the weaknesses in his life," Jill said. "In fact, he encourages feedback from me. Pat has learned that I can stand back and evaluate his effectiveness with the children and other endeavors. Mayor Ed Koch of New York City is famous for his greeting, 'Hey, how'm I doing?'

"I haven't always been able to take constructive criticism from Jill, though," I admitted.

"Maybe that's because I haven't always known how to give criticism.

"When sharing weaknesses with Pat, there are two points I've learned that I must observe. I must guard against a critical spirit, and there must be true appreciation for the good that is operating in his life.

"If I come to Pat with an attitude that flows from a bitter, hurting spirit, he recognizes my fault at once. This immediately puts him on the defensive. A shield rises that's as impenetrable as an iron warship."

"I know what you mean," Richard said. "There's a secretary at work named Lois. She's a Christian, but there aren't many people who like her. Lois is constantly analyzing everyone she comes in contact with. She's testing their spirituality and their performance. I'm uncomfortable around her.''

"That's it," Jill said. "When I come to Pat with my feedback, there must be a humble attitude that's been bathed in prayer. True appreciation comes by a continual search for the things that are right in Pat's personality. While I may feel that Pat is off base in a section of his life, I still want to show him the personal warmth and respect that he is due because of all the things that are dead-center correct.''

"In *Western Theology* (Pioneer Vent, 1985)," I added, as an illustration, "Wes Seeliger gives a colorful analogy of the pastor's role within the Church. This same picture can be used to describe the position of a husband as the pastor of his small flock, the family. Seelinger sees the pastor as the cook in a cattle drive. With a unique function, unlike the other cowboys, he is nevertheless on an equal footing with the rest. Without confusing his position with the trail boss (God), the cook's job is to provide the others with the necessary food that will enable them to do their work. Ephesians 4 says that pastors and the other ministers in the body are to equip the Church for works of service.

"When a husband and wife understand what true headship means in the marriage relationship, they can begin to cooperate with each other in new ways. Each husband is blessed with unique talents and interests. He will bring to the family his brand of humor and cultural complexities.''

"As a counterbalance," Jill inserted, "God has ordained that the wife complement her husband in the areas where he may be lacking. But more important, she is commissioned to encourage him to see the many possibilities born in each member of the family. Her intuitive nature can perceive his strengths and encourage them.''

With surprising tenderness, Richard said, "I believe that as a husband and wife start to search for ways to confide in each other, a depth of understanding will develop which will equip the entire family with talents and skills to serve each other and the community around them.''

"Are you saying that a man will lose his need to dominate if his wife can help him be secure in his position as head of the household?" Crystal asked.

"Yep," I agreed, "and that applies directly to ANOINT and beginning to **Notice Your Partner's Needs.**"

"But," Jill interrupted, "there's also the fact that the man must be sensitive to his wife's hurts, needs, and desires."

"Are your needs a great deal different from mine?" Richard asked Crystal.

"Probably not. I don't have the same desire to be the head of our household because God hasn't given me that place, but I do have a need to have the kind of confidence shown in my opinions that your parents showed to you last week. In fact, I hope we don't have to wait until we are sixty years old before you realize that my thoughts and ideas can be of value, too," Crystal said without any defensiveness.

"Crystal," Richard asked, "what are your most basic needs?"

Jill and I looked at each other with wonder. It appeared that all of Richard's defensiveness had been left in Atlanta. We saw wisdom, tenderness, and openness coming from him that would have been unbelievable only a week before.

Crystal started to pick at her fingernails. "I don't want to have to tell you. I want you to know."

Because Jill understood her confusion, she said, "Crystal, remember that Richard isn't a woman. There will always be things that he won't be able to see that seem extremely apparent to you. You have to tell him your needs."

Picking up a napkin from the center of the table, Crystal looked at Richard and said, "The first thing that I need we have already talked about. I need you to value my opinions. I also need you to approach me with romance," Crystal said in a rather matter-of-fact manner.

"Crystal, I try to be a good lover."

"I'm not talking about sex." The volume of Crystal's voice rose, and there was a definite edge in the tone.

"What are you talking about, then?" Richard asked, striving successfully not to match her harshness.

"I think we can tell you, Richard," I said. "Jill and I have bumped through this argument enough times to sink an island." As we had anticipated, Richard had not grasped the meaning of romance as it applies to a woman. Now was the time to share with him in greater detail how a woman feels about love and intimacy.

"There must be a barrier erected for the woman," Jill said, "protecting her from the hassle of the outside world before she can respond to a man sexually. Women call that barrier of protection romance. There is a great deal of stress, strain, lots of decisions, and hard work in her day. Too often sex becomes another responsibility for a woman, rather than a joy."

"I could not understand what Jill was saying until one day I listened to Dr. Donald Joy on the "Focus on the Family" radio program. Dr. Joy is professor of human development at Asbury Theological Seminary in Wilmore, Kentucky. He noted the twelve steps that appear to characterize courtship in virtually all societies. His source for those stages is the book *Intimate Behavior* by Desmond Morris (Random House, 1971). As you will see, they are progressively more intimate in contact. In most successful relationships, it is the man who initiates all the moves forward from one step to the next. However, it is the woman who is most likely to be wounded by a man's forwardness or a broken relationship.

"Once the trust of a woman has been violated, it is difficult for her to bounce back. The steps of intimacy may have to begin all over again in order for the wounds to be healed."

With care to specific details, I shared the twelve steps to intimacy. They are as follows:

1. *Eye to body*
When we glance at a person, we can tell much about him or her—sex, size, shape, age, personality, and status. Attraction depends on the importance people place on these initial, determining criteria. These are not always shallow assessments, and most of us would do well to attend to those first impressions.

2. Eye to eye

Dr. Joy says, "When the man and woman exchange glances, their most natural reaction is to look away, usually with embarrassment. If their eyes meet again, they may smile, which signals that they might like to become better acquainted."

3. Voice to voice

Initial conversation is always trivial. Questions like "Did I meet you in Alabama?" "What is your name?" "Where do you live?" The questions gradually become more intimate by nature. This is a long period, and the two people learn much about each other. If they are compatible in their interests, habits, hobbies, likes and dislikes, they will become friends.

4. Hand to hand

The first instance of physical contact is almost without exception nonromantic. He helps her into a car or up a flight of stairs. At this point either one of the people can withdraw from the relationship without rejecting the other. If hand-to-hand contact continues, however, it will eventually become evidence of the couple's romantic attachment to each other.

5. Hand to shoulder

"This affectionate embrace is still noncommittal," according to Dr. Joy. "It is a 'buddy' type position in which the man and woman are side-by-side. They are more concerned with the world in front of them than they are with each other. The hand to shoulder contact reveals a relationship that is more than a close friendship, but probably not real love."

6. Hand to waist

This is where the rubber meets the road. It is clearly romantic. Two normal people of the same sex would not do this. Hand-to-waist contact indicates the couple is close enough to be sharing secrets and intimate language with each other. Yet, they are still walking side-by-side and looking forward at the world.

7. Face to face

Dr. Joy explains, "This level of contact involves gazing into one another's eyes, hugging and kissing. If none of the previous steps were skipped, the man and woman will have developed a special code from experience that enables them to engage in deep communication with very few words. At this point sexual desire becomes an important factor in the relationship.''

8. *Hand to head*

An extension of the previous stage, the man and woman cradle or stroke each other's head while kissing or talking.

The last four stages are distinctly sexual and private. They are:

9. *Hand to body*

10. *Mouth to breast*

11. *Touching below the waist*

12. *Intercourse*

"Obviously," Dr. Joy asserts, "the last three steps of physical contact should be reserved for the marriage relationship, particularly since they are immensely and progressively emotional—especially for the woman.''

Dr. Joy believes that any couple contemplating marriage should make their courtship long. They should proceed through each step slowly because of the physical bonding which is taking place. Patience through the first levels will assure that the last steps after the wedding will be more enjoyable for the couple.

"It is a mistake to rush the relationship, skip steps and become intimate too quickly," Dr. Joy warns. "Impatience can damage intimacy and reduce the possibility of a solid, enduring union.

"Couples who feel they have rushed these steps may find it helpful to retrace them and thereby experience a better physical relationship," Joy asserts.

Richard and Crystal laughed. "Believe me," Richard said, "we observed the first five steps in the beginning of our relationship down to the last gnat's tailfeather.''

"Richard was extremely shy when we were courting," Crystal said.

"And you were the most standoffish girl I'd ever met."

"That's the kind of romance I want back in our lives," Crystal said.

"Is it possible?" Richard asked Pat.

"Not only is it possible, but it is essential for a woman to feel loved and secure," I assured Richard.

"On the radio program, Dr. Joy referred to material from *The Tangled Wing: Biological Constraint on the Human Spirit,* by Melvin Konner (Holt, Rinehart and Winston, 1982). It appears that even animals go through the same courtship procedures.

"In fact, we could learn a lot from the animal kingdom."

Richard put his arm around Crystal and joked, "That's what I keep telling her."

"Dr. Joy mentioned that in Konner's book he explains that 85 percent of animals, birds, and humans are not perfectly bonded, because the male in the species tends to be competitive and oriented toward 'tournaments.' "

I explained that Konner's book includes a checklist giving conditions of the ideal pair-bonding for birds, animals, and humans. These are:

1. Male and female mature sexually at about the same age.

2. Male and female are about the same size, without differentiating ornamentation. (For example: In the bird kingdom, when the male and female are hard to differentiate, there is a better bonding.)

3. Males do not compete for paired females, showing respect for other bonds.

4. Males are not dominating, and marriages are not "chain of command" in structure.

5. Male and female engage in a long, elaborate courtship.

6. "Nest building" precedes breeding.

7. Male and female are bonded not only sexually, but socially, and are always seen together.

8. Males show a high investment in the care, feeding, and training of their offspring.

"By its very nature," Dr. Joy concludes, "perfect pair-bonding is lifelong, exclusive, and perpetually intimate."

"All right," Richard said, aggravated by his inability to understand how all of this bonding related to him and Crystal. "Crystal and I did all that. What's wrong now?"

Jill smiled, "Richard, Crystal wants this kind of bonding every time you have sex."

Crystal nodded in agreement. Richard threw up his hands in exasperation. "That could take hours!" he said.

"But, Richard," Crystal said in a voice so sweet it almost melted the windowpanes. "I promise I could make it worth your time."

As Richard's eyeballs steamed, Andrea and Sarah popped open the front door. "We're ready for lunch," they announced.

It had been a good morning. As Pat and I waved to Crystal, Richard, and their girls while they pulled away from the driveway, both of us said in chorus, "Can you believe the change in them?"

Chapter Fifteen

Will This Take Forever?

During the next week, Richard was called out of town on business to the corporate headquarters of the company with which his firm was merging. Crystal packed a lunch and little Kara, the baby she was watching, into her car and wound her way across town to one of the parks surrounding a lake.

Crystal explained to me later that she didn't mind Richard's absence because she understood that he was at the edge of an exciting opportunity within the structure of his company. Everything seemed to point to his being able to form and head a new division which would utilize the handicapped. The extra time alone would also give her a few additional hours to prepare for the Sunday school class she and Richard co-sponsor.

However, as she sat in a hot car waiting for the never-ending stream of traffic to pass, an uneasy stirring seemed to fill her mind and spirit. Quite unexpectedly, it didn't seem fair to her that Richard was traveling to exciting places, staying in plush hotels, and eating in expensive restaurants while she was stuck at home with no one to entertain her.

The car glided easily into the parking lot east of the park

area. Crystal stared straight ahead for such a long time that Kara started to wiggle and cry because she wanted to get out of her car seat.

Crystal was watching Kara dig in the sand, when a young man approached her. Crystal recognized him immediately as the attendant at the gas station she and Richard frequented. The owner is a member of our church.

The "misplaced" attendant smiled and spoke in a pleasant southern accent, "Crystal, would you mind watchin' my things for a bit?" He threw his car keys, wallet, and a frayed towel on her blanket, assuming that her answer was yes.

Crystal was unexpectedly flushed and flattered by the fact that this handsome young swimmer eight or ten years her junior had taken the steps to learn her name. With an uncharacteristic lack of discipline, her mind wandered when she tried to concentrate on the now uninteresting study book that lay in her lap.

A secret, simple fantasy pleasantly formed in her mind. She imagined the young man watching her while she pumped gas, waiting for her to come into the station. He had fought the temptation, but he desired more than anything to establish a relationship with her.

The daydreaming continued as Crystal gave up on her book and quietly drew in the sand. Her reverie was broken by the young man's laughter as he teased Kara. Suddenly, Crystal was jolted from her ridiculous fantasy. She looked at the tall, strikingly handsome man standing over Kara, mopping his face and shoulders.

"My name is John," he turned to face her, wiped the excess moisture from his hand, and extended it to her. "You can't imagine how happy I am to see you. I've wanted to talk with you for a long time." With an explosion of sentences, the youth talked with an openness, freedom, even abandonment that Crystal had rarely seen in men twice his age, much less someone barely past eighteen.

"Brad, who owns the station, has told me a lot about your church, and I'm interested in knowing more. Do you think that we could maybe meet sometime and talk about God, the church, and other things? I've got a lot of questions, and everybody who comes into the station from your church seems to look up to you.

"I've been watching you for months now and I'm impressed, too. You have an air of goodness and sweetness . . . but strength. I'd like to learn from the best, and from what I've seen, you're the best.

"Would you be willing to teach me?" The young man stooped down as he looked directly into Crystal's eyes. Her stomach gave a pleasant flip when he smiled at her. "A weekly class to start off with, and then if we get along, we could meet a couple of times a week."

Crystal was flattered. Perhaps God had sent this young man. She had often prayed for him as he moved around the pumps and equipment. Of course, Crystal had placed no large significance on him; she always prayed for the people who served her in stores and restaurants. For a few seconds, she was ready to agree to meet him—maybe the church would have a spare room.

Then Crystal's mind leaped back to the uneasy feelings she had experienced driving to the beach. She remembered her casual thoughts about how unfair her life had become. The past months had not been easy. Now, it appeared that she and Richard were finally on the road to a good marriage. As though God was placing a massive yellow caution flag in front of her face, she was aware of her vulnerable emotional position. This was no time for her to be seeing another man—especially one who was young, handsome, easy to talk with, and interested in her.

Crystal thanked him. "You could come over to supper one night. Richard and I could talk with you," Crystal said, as disappointment spread over his expectant face.

"I really wanted to learn from *you*," he insisted.

"You can learn from both of us. We're a pretty good team."

"Okay," John said, no longer disappointed. "Let's set up a time."

The dinner engagement could never be worked out. However,

the next Sunday John came to church and gave his heart to the Lord.

On Tuesday, Crystal came over to the house and told me about the incident at the park. She didn't deceive herself that John was interested in her as a woman. On the other hand, Crystal had to admit that she was interested in the world of sexual fantasy he represented.

"Will I ever be really satisified?" Crystal asked me. "The thoughts I had at the park were those of a silly schoolgirl. I love Richard. I don't want to be involved in some fantasy world."

"The world of the afternoon soap opera?" I laughed.

"Exactly. What's wrong with me? Do I want to sabotage my marriage?"

"Don't be too hard on yourself, Crystal," I encouraged her. "Healing the past hurts will take time."

"Will it take forever?"

"I can guarantee you that it won't take forever. Though there will always be room for improvement in your relationship with Richard. Remember, it will take time and action for old wounds to be healed."

"What are some of the things you've found that helped you?"

"I've thought about that a lot, Crystal. I believe that God has shown me four specific areas in which I needed a spiritual overhaul.

"First, *I was not able to see Pat's weaknesses as they really were*. In the areas where he was inadequate, I took on the attitude that Pat had dealt me a personal shutout.

"During the first years of our marriage, Pat was a man unable to express emotion or share deep feelings. I refused to comprehend that this was his personality flaw. Instead I campaigned as though it were my problem. I felt a sense of aloneness because we weren't emotionally on equal ground. There was continual frustration because he wouldn't share himself with me.

"My question was constantly, 'What can I DO to make him share with me?' The answer was nothing. But I refused to allow it to rest. He *would* change, and I would see to it."

One of Crystal's eyebrows raised slightly, as she said, "I've done that often enough. It really does seem foolish when you think about it, though.''

"Second, *I could not release Pat*. By not seeing his unique personality flaws, I was not able to release him to become the person God intended him to be.

"I felt that I knew best how Pat should develop emotionally. I would orchestrate his actions and motives to meet my needs. That had far-reaching physical and emotional implications.

"It was like the 'boy/girl' theory. The boy wants the girl because he can't have her. When he wins her, he doesn't want her anymore. By demanding that Pat let me into his inner being, I was actually driving him away. When I insisted, screamed, or manipulated, he became more withdrawn and perplexed.

"Pat admits that he felt that if he gave himself to me, there would be no end to it. He never sat down and analyzed his thoughts, but he came to view me like an enormous Venus's flytrap. If he got too close, I would catch him, totally envelop him, and absorb him slowly into my personality.

"Third, *in my mind, I made Pat responsible for my flaws,* and I made him responsible for the parts of my personality which were weak and insecure.

"I told him in a thousand different ways at a hundred different volumes that I couldn't be whole without his help. My happiness and contentment were wrapped up in his ability to perform to my specification. Unlike Paul, I could not learn to be content in whatever condition I found myself. My contentment came from Pat. My joy was wrapped in a package with his name on it.

"While I knew that I didn't want Pat to provide for my every single need, I could not adequately convey that to him. The more I wanted, the less he could respond.

"I realize now that my insecurities were *my* insecurities and Pat would never be able to heal them. Eleanor Roosevelt once said, 'No one can make you feel inferior without your consent.'

"Jesus is my healer and helper. He is the one who gives me joy and happiness—not Pat or any other man.

"Fourth, *the task which I presented to Pat, of being everything to me, was impossible.* Therefore, I set him up to fail. No matter what his successes in the outside world, he could never be a successful person because I wanted everything from him.

"In the Psalms, God warns the Israelites over and over about looking to other nations for help in battle. In facing my personal war, I tried to make a daily contract with Pat to obtain the horses and chariots I needed to wage my inner conflicts.

"At times, Pat would give me a token rose and a night out as an Egyptian horse, but it was never enough.

"Someone has written a 'Green Thumb' for marriage—asserting that a lasting relationship is like a garden. Tend it lovingly and it will give you bountiful rewards. I keep a copy on my refrigerator. Amazingly, it coincides with our marital strengths and weaknesses:

1. Provide a nourishing environment.
2. Know your partner.
3. Adapt to change.
4. Deal promptly with minor problems.
5. Give each other room.
6. Plan for the future.
7. Acknowledge your commitment.

"Over the years, Pat and I have learned to recognize flawed areas in our personalities. We bring them to the Lord for an overhaul. With His help and mutual encouragement, we are making progress in dealing with them.

"I no longer take responsibility for the things in Pat's life where God is dealing and leading. I don't force him to be everything for me. He, in turn, has learned to deal with the hard areas in his personality that kept significant relationships at arm's length. His becoming open and honest with me didn't mean the destruction of his personality but the development of sensitivity, which has made him a better person.

"We are still in the process of helping each other to come to our fullest potential, and that isn't always without struggle. But we are no longer pulling at opposite ends of the rope, each insisting that the other release his end first."

"Jill, I also need to deal with the guilt I feel about what happened at the lake," Crystal said.

"The first thing you need to do is forgive yourself for the feelings which were stirred inside of you at the park. He is a handsome young man . . ."

". . . and it's been such a long time since a man looked at me as he did. I confess, I loved the way he smiled right into my eyes. Then later, I hated myself for enjoying it."

"That's the second step. You need to learn to be honest with yourself and your feelings—as honest as you've been today. Confess your sin and repent.

"Crystal, realize that the battle isn't over. It will take time, but the goal is worth the effort. Above all, train your mind to remember the good times you and Richard have had. Don't always dwell on the negative. Think about the special times."

"Over the past two weeks, whenever I've gotten discouraged I have remembered what happened here two weeks ago on Saturday, when we had our breakfast together and Richard was tender and vulnerable with me.

"Jill, there has been a change in Richard. Everything isn't totally different, but I know he's trying. If that young man had come up to me six months ago, I'd have jumped at the chance to get to know him. Thank God for the changes that have been made in our lives.

"I'm going to write down the three things you suggested," Crystal said, looking for a pencil and paper, "which will help me take time and action. First, I need to forgive myself. Then confess my sin, openly and honestly. Third, I should train my mind to think about the good things in Richard and in our marriage. That seems simple enough."

"One last thing," I said. "Miracles are terrific, but a gradual healing in a relationship is equally as wonderful."

I knew that we had all been changed through the hard months that Richard and Crystal had struggled in their marriage. Pat and I had grown, and we had seen significant changes in Crystal and Richard's lives.

There was a long pause. Not uneasy, but the kind of silence that's comfortable with friends. Crystal broke the stillness. "We're going to make it. I know that now. Thank you, Jill. You've become a good friend."

Chapter Sixteen

Take Time, Take Action

After Richard came home from his business trip, he was politely invited, then mildly coerced by Stephen and Thomas to attend their first baseball game of the new season. The sun had not yet burned off the morning fog as we settled onto the bleachers to wait for the Saturday morning Little League game to commence. The other parents and friends of the players had gathered into a tight cluster on the other side of the bleachers. With the clamor of a few enthusiastic parents cheering, Richard and I had almost complete privacy.

"It's taken me months, but I'm beginning to understand what damage I've done to Crystal emotionally. I'd forgotten what an exciting person she really is. As I've taken the steps to love her unconditionally, the sparkle of laughter is slowly coming back. That familiar mischievous edge is inching into her humor again," Richard confided to me.

"It's going to take time for her to heal. Healing is a process; it almost never comes instantly," I said, seconds before I shouted encouragement to Thomas, who was running to catch a fly ball. After the ball was securely back in the glove of the pitcher, I added, "There are several steps to healing emotional wounds, and the first one is to realize that there are no quick cures."

"I would give anything to be able to dust away Crystal's past pain the way we scraped the dirt and crumbs off our benches this morning."

"If you rush the process, though, you're likely to end up with only a scab over the wound. The months that Jill took to heal were the most painful in my life. Even now, though it's been years, a slight remark can reveal the hurt again.

"In his book, *Becoming a Friend and Lover*, Dick Purnell warned that the healing of emotional wounds takes time," I shared with Richard, "but we can't passively wait for time alone to accomplish healing. We must play a role in the healing process. Otherwise, a scar may form and the area will be sensitive to the touch, or it could produce a festering sore underneath the skin which could spread poison throughout the body."

"**Take time and action.** That's the last step in ANOINT, isn't it?" Richard asked.

"Yes, and the final part of our plan could be the most important step for your marriage. Don't be impatient, even though you want the vivacious young woman you married back and you want her now."

"How can I encourage the process along?" Richard asked.

"Perhaps the most important thing you can do is to allow Jesus to help in the healing. Look out there on that ball field. Last spring most of those boys didn't know second base from home plate. Now they're playing the game like they invented it."

At that moment the batter hit a pop fly. The ball landed squarely in the glove of the second baseman, who allowed it to drop through his hands to the ground. As four of the boys fumbled to retrieve it, Richard and I laughed. "Well, with some exceptions," I said, "they can play the game. Yet even with the fumbles, we don't call the boys failures and vow never to let them play again. We cheer them on and encourage them until they are finally able to play. That's the way God encourages us. He is pleased with each step we take. He initiated healing in the first place. Isaiah 53:4, 5 (NIV) says, 'Surely he took up our infirmities and carried our sorrows . . . and by his wounds we are healed.' Because Jesus understands the depth of the hurts, He can help Crystal become whole again.

"The third thing you can do is help Crystal face and release her emotions. By your listening to her, she will be able to walk through much of the pains of the past. She needs to identify hidden feelings. You'll find that as you allow her to share her pain with you, you'll become better able to identify your own painful areas.

"Listening is never easy for a man. Nevertheless, it's essential for a woman. Last week, Jill was involved in a real estate training class. This was something she had wanted to do for a long time. We made arrangements for someone to pick up the children and we all pitched in with the housework. The first night she came home from the eight-hour class, Jill wanted to tell me about the entire day.

"I know it's important to her to be able to tell me about the details. After about a half hour of listening, however, I lost interest and I let her know that I wanted her to finish the story quickly. Jill was hurt. She needed to be able to vent her emotions of the day. I didn't allow her that opportunity. Perhaps there is no way men can really understand the depth of a woman's need to share."

"I can do a lot better than I have in the past, though," Richard interjected.

By now the game was over. We piled the boys into the car, and I picked up Purnell's book from the backseat. "The next step is to ask God to show you ways that He can use the hurts of the past for good. Dick Purnell wrote, 'We don't have to continue to live in despair or guilt. In God, we can have true hope and can move forward to be used by Him to help others.

" 'Our lives may be a scrap pile, but God can build trophies from scrap piles. To gain God's perspective on your wounds, keep an eye out for how He has used and can use your pain and failures and wounds for good.' "

"The last step is to strive for intimacy with Crystal," I said, flipping the pages of Purnell's book to another marked section. I read, 'I [Purnell] define intimacy as total life sharing—sharing your life completely with someone else. It includes being open to and deeply involved in the inner and outer life of another person by seeking to understand all of the aspects that make up that person. Intimacy is a process, not a once-for-all accomplishment. Each of us is developing, growing, learning, and aging in all aspects of our lives. Life is a constant flux, so intimacy, if it is in a healthy state, is not static but constantly developing and growing too.' "

"I've seen, through you and Jill, that marriage is worth the work that it involves," Richard confessed.

"Jill and I don't pretend to be perfect, but things are better than they were a few years ago. We are striving to be the partners that God desires us to be and that our marriage deserves."

I pulled the car into the traffic and headed for home. There had been an accident on the freeway, and we were stuck in one spot for a good fifteen minutes before we started to inch our way again. "This is an appropriate ending to our morning," Richard said. "Even getting home is going to take time."

"Yeah, but not too much time, if I take the appropriate action," I said, wheeling the car into the next lane and heading for the exit. Within fifteen minutes we were at Richard's house.

"Thanks for the demonstration of *Take Time, Take Action*," Richard said. "I figure we got home an hour earlier than we would have if we'd stayed on the interstate highway. Let's hope taking appropriate action helps in our relationship as much as it helps in traffic."

Chapter Seventeen

The Last Hurrah

One Sunday morning after church, Crystal and Richard came up to us, hand in hand. Crystal was wearing her hair down; she looked like a teenager. Richard had on a new suit to match his new professional image. Now that he had the responsibility of forming a new division for the handicapped in a large corporation, he would be meeting challenges that were completely different.

"Pat, we need at least one more session with the two of you," Richard said. "Let us take you out to dinner—no crisis—only a good time."

"The whole family?" I asked as Michael swung from my pant leg.

"No. Only the two of you."

We made a date for Friday evening. After dinner had been served, Richard said, "Pat, I'm interested to know how you realized that a change had to be made in your marriage."

"In December of 1982," I explained, "Jill calmly announced that she would rather be anywhere in the world than to be married to me. I had not known the signs to watch for that would have told me Jill was horribly dissatisfied with our marriage. In fact, I was pleased that for the last few months, things had been going so well for a change. Jill had stopped fighting with me. I felt Jill had at last begun to mature.''

"The last big fight that Pat and I had was in the early fall,'' Jill added as she took a sip of her water. "Starting with a nag, I ended up screaming at him. Pat responded in his usual calm manner, hardly lifting an eyebrow. He had concluded years before that it did no good for both of us to scream. Also, Pat isn't the type of person to raise his voice, no matter how much he is provoked. I think he has only yelled at me two times during our entire marriage.

" 'Are you listening to me?' I screamed, desperate to get his attention. Pat didn't look up from the sports section. 'Do you hear what I'm saying?'

"In my mind I felt that Pat didn't even care enough about me to argue. I became more angry than before, 'Look at me,' I shrieked. I felt that I knew what he was thinking when his eyes finally did meet mine. Even though he didn't say a word, I responded to the unasked question in his eye, 'Don't look at me with that smug attitude. I didn't used to be this way. You've driven me to be a screaming shrew.' ''

"Unfortunately I laughed and asked her, 'Do you like being this way?' ''

" 'What else can I do? You made me this way,' '' I shrieked.

"In a disgusted, emotionless monotone, I responded to Jill's outburst, 'Okay, it's my fault. I'm sorry. Can we please drop it now?'

"Though I'd not known it at the time, I had spoken the truth. Pat had made me into the woman I was—screaming, manipulative, angry. But I had also made him into the man he was—unconcerned, aloof, unresponsive,'' Jill added.

"In December 1987 *USA Today* published a list of gripes men have against women. One of them was that women don't understand investments. Men often think in terms of material investment. But they miss knowing that a good wife is the greatest investment any man can have in his life. Family expert and author Tim LaHaye says that a wife is the best investment a man can have. Everything he invests in her will be paid back in abundance and blessing,'' I told them.

"The women countered with gripes of their own. They felt that men are emotionally inferior to women; they can't admit that they are wrong; and they have egos as fragile as a newborn's skull,'' Jill said.

I shared that Dr. James Dobson has written, ''With regard to your husband, my advice is that you change that which can be altered, explain that which can be understood, teach that which can be learned, resolve that which can be improved, resolve that which can be settled and negotiate that which is open to compromise.''

"If there was that much wrong with your marriage, what kept the whole thing going for over ten years?'' Crystal asked.

"One of the big pluses in our marriage relationship was that Jill was able to create an atmosphere which made me totally comfortable and secure with her love. I knew that she not only loved me but that she liked me as well. I didn't worry that she would run off and ditch me some day. She had given herself to me completely and I knew that,'' I explained.

"While I never recognized the positive gestures she was making which made me happy and secure, they were there looming in the foreground of every day that we were together. It was the little things she did that told me that I was more important to her than her career, her parents, or her church.

"First, *she always complimented me and built me up in front of other people.* I never had to wonder or be concerned about what she might do to me when we ministered together. I never dreaded trips to visit her family in fear that she might expose some ridiculous mistake I'd made. I didn't have any dark secrets, but there were incidents and conflicts which I preferred to leave under wraps. Jill never exposed my naked, vulnerable areas to the world.

"There is a well-known author, pastor, and speaker who takes one continual potshot after another at his wife. Though it's always done with good-humored jesting, I've often wondered what his wife must think while she sits in the audience, listening to her faults and foibles being exposed to the listening public.

"Second, *Jill was willing from the beginning of our marriage to take up the slack when I couldn't or wouldn't see a need.* On our honeymoon, I left her to carry the luggage while I went off to find out some earth-shattering sporting fact."

I explained before that Jill decorated our homes without my input or encouragement. She entertained my clients and friends with style and grace. I showed up and became the lord and master of the party, but I never helped with the mountain of dirty dishes afterward.

She disciplined our children, month after month, without ever saying, "Wait until your father gets home. You'll get it then." Yet in the larger areas of real or potential crisis, she always consulted me, valued my judgment, and insisted that my advice be observed.

"This leads me to the *third* thing Jill did that made me secure with her," I said. "*She always acknowledged in words and actions that I was head of the household.* At times, even now, I can be unaware of the hurts and feelings of people I interact with on a regular basis. While I've tried to zero in on meeting Jill's needs, there are others that I come in contact with who are sometimes hurt by my abrupt mannerisms.

"Jill has never made it a point to embarrass me during those times when I've been less than courteous. Without complaint or discouragement, her attitude says, 'Pat is my head and I'm proud of him.' Taking up the slack in my weakened personality never meant that Jill took over my position. I knew that I was secure with her and I rested in that security.

"Fourth, *she was willing to leave everything to be with me.* Can you imagine the shock and surprise of a young woman who had always lived in a large, urban area in the Midwest being told one day that she was to be transported to the heart of the South because I had been offered a new job? I had given her no warning. She had no idea that my job in Chicago was not secure.

"Jill never flinched. She knew that her place was with me, and she started making immediate plans. If Jill ever shed a tear about having to move from her home and family, I never knew about it. Sure, she would miss them; and of course, it meant the breaking of some major family bonds, but her face was set toward Atlanta.

"Jill instinctively knew what Dr. Ed Wheat wrote about in his book *Love-Life for Every Married Couple.* 'We must understand, first of all, that marriage begins with a *leaving:* leaving all other relationships. The closest relationship outside of marriage is specified here, implying that if it is necessary to leave your father and mother, then certainly all lesser ties must be broken, changed, or left behind.' "

"That does seem to be hard for many women," Richard agreed. "There is an amazingly talented young man I've become acquainted with in the home office of the new corporation. He is totally stifled in his job. He is unhappy because he must constantly mediate between his division chief, who should be retired, and the workers who are on the construction site.

"The stress he lives under is almost beyond comprehension. His position and professional reputation are constantly being threatened. When he was offered a position as general manager with the new company, he saw it as the answer to his and his wife's prayers.

"However, his wife had other ideas. She refused to move. How could he ask her to leave everything dear to her—her friends, the church, and the children's school? His well-being as a man and provider is under constant jeopardy, but she will not budge from her nest of security."

"Jill understood the need to leave everything and follow me. That made a huge difference in our marriage.

"Fifth, *she was always involved in my interests.* Jill wanted to go to the games and be a part of my life. She could talk intelligently about basketball and quote statistics as well as any man.

"Sixth, *Jill was the first one to point out a concern in our relationship.* She took the admonition, 'Do not let the sun go down on your wrath,' seriously. While I wanted to hide my head in a column of sporting figures, Jill didn't want even the slightest hurt to go unmended. I realize now that many wounds were bound and covered by her ability to quickly identify a problem area and insist on a resolution."

By now a wonderful smile had overtaken the expression on Jill's face. "I had no idea that you've been this observant—that you would know the things I was doing that were right in our marriage."

"Six years ago I couldn't have given you one thing that you had done right. Not that I didn't know there were things. It was simply that I was completely out of touch with my emotions and the important things going on in our home. The Lord has made me aware that not only must a wife appreciate and like her husband to find fulfillment, but a husband is personally enriched when he learns to love his wife."

After we left Richard and Crystal at their door, Jill looked me in the eye and said, "Thank you."

I took her hand and asked, "For what?"

"For being you."

We pulled into the driveway of our house, and I put my arm around her shoulder. "You've made it much easier for me to expose myself and to know how I really feel." I got out of the car and went around to open Jill's door.

As we walked to the doorway, I slipped my arm around her waist and whispered, "We're now at number six in Dr. Joy's steps to bonding."

"It's not romantic to count, Williams," Jill said in feigned irritation.

"I know, but it's so much fun," I said as I brushed away a stray curl from her face.